The Lucent Library of Historical Eras

The 1960s
Arts and Entertainment

Stuart A. Kallen

LUCENT BOOKS®

THOMSON

GALE

San Diego • Detroit • New York • San Francisco • Cleveland • New Haven, Conn. • Waterville, Maine • London • Munich

LIBRARY OF CONGRESS CATALOGING-IN-PUBLICATION DATA

Kallen, Stuart A., 1955-
  Arts and entertainment / by Stuart A. Kallen.
    p. cm. — (Lucent library of historical eras. 1960's)
Summary: Analyzes the revolution which took place in such areas as writing, movies,
television, commercial art, and music in the nineteen sixties.
Includes bibliographical references and index.
  ISBN 1-59018-388-6 (hardback : alk. paper)
  1. Arts, American—20th century—Juvenile literature. 2. Nineteen sixties—Juvenile
literature. [1. Arts. 2. Nineteen sixties.] I. Title. II. Series.
  NX504.K337 2004
  700'.973'09046—dc22
                           2003019651

Contents

Foreword

Looking back from the vantage point of the present, history can be viewed as a myriad of intertwining roads paved by human events. Some paths stand out—broad highways whose mileposts, even from a distance of centuries, are clear. The events that propelled the rise to power of Germany's Third Reich, its role in World War II, and its eventual demise, for example, are well defined and documented.

Other roads are less distinct, their route sometimes hidden from view. Modern legislatures may have developed from old tribal councils, for example, but the links between them are indistinct in places, open to discussion and interpretation.

The architecture of civilization—law, religion, art, science, and government—as well as the more everyday aspects of our culture—what we eat, what we wear—all developed along the historical roads and byways. In that progression can be traced every facet of modern life.

A broad look back along these roads reveals that many paths—though of vastly different character—seem to converge at a few critical junctions. These intersections are those great historical eras that echo over the long, steady course of human history, extending beyond the past and into the present.

These epic periods of time are the focus of Lucent's Library of Historical Eras. They shine through the mists of history like beacons, illuminated by a burst of creativity that propels events forward—so bright that we, from thousands of years away, can clearly see the chain of events leading to the present.

Each Lucent Library of Historical Eras consists of a set of books that highlight various aspects of these major eras. For example, the Elizabethan England library features volumes on Queen Elizabeth I and her court, Elizabethan theater, the great playwrights, and everyday life in Elizabethan London.

The mini-library approach allows for the division of each era into its most significant and most interesting parts and the exploration of those parts in depth. Also, social and cultural trends as well as illustrative documents and eyewitness accounts can be prominently featured in individual volumes.

Lucent's Library of Historical Eras presents a wealth of information to young readers. The lively narrative, fully documented primary and secondary source quotations, maps, photographs, sidebars, and annotated bibliographies serve as launching points for class discussion and further research.

In studying the great historical eras, students also develop a better understanding of our own times. What we learn from the past and how we apply it in the present may shape the future and may determine whether our era will be a guiding light to those traveling future roads.

Introduction:
Revolution in the Arts

The 1960s was one of the most turbulent decades in American history, politically, socially, and culturally. Tens of thousands of American soldiers were killed—and many thousands more were wounded—in an unpopular war in Vietnam. Between 1965 and 1969, race riots erupted nearly every summer in many American inner cities. Students protesting the Vietnam War and government responses to poverty and other social ills clashed violently with police on college campuses and in the streets. Many young people called for outright revolution and openly urged the overthrow of the U.S. government. Millions of middle-class teenagers abandoned the values of their parents' generation and began to experiment with psychedelic drugs and casual sex. The women's rights movement led millions of Americans to question their traditional roles and demand more control over reproduction along with equality at work and at home.

In the midst of this turbulence, authors, artists, musicians, playwrights, and filmmakers were producing brilliant creations of historic importance. Inspired and exhilarated by the political and social protests that marked the decade, these creative people used their work to loudly question conventional wisdom, popular opinion, and rules of all kinds. More than a reflection of rebellious times, the art and popular pastimes of the 1960s fueled further rebellion, becoming both cause and effect in this no-limits era.

Authors wrote best-selling books that covered difficult topics such as violence, war, racism, sexism, and sex. Singers and songwriters scornfully questioned American cultural values, sang of universal love, and even issued calls for revolution. Provocative dramas and films dealt with formerly forbidden subjects such as interracial romance, free love, the horrors of war, and the perceived joys of the counterculture lifestyle.

The sixties, of course, were not the first time that creative people broke with tradition and mainstream society. Challenging the status quo has been a time-honored role for artists throughout history. In the 1960s, however, the mass marketing of books, music, and television allowed a small group of artists to spread their messages to nearly everyone who cared to see or hear it. And for the first time, mainstream publishers and producers disseminated revolutionary tracts in stores throughout the Western world.

Mass Consumption of Revolutionary Art

Many revolutionary artists and entertainers of the 1960s were part of the postwar baby boom generation. This population "bubble" of 75 million men and women born between 1946 and 1964 dominated nearly every aspect of American culture. In 1964, seventeen-year-olds composed the largest age group in the United States. By 1966, almost 50 percent of all people in America were under the age of twenty-six. That meant that groundbreaking art and entertainment created by young people found a ready market of like-minded young consumers. And baby boom Americans were some of the richest people in history; the average suburban teenager in the 1960s had more disposable income than a family of four in 1940.

Baby boomers were also the best-educated generation in history, attending college in unprecedented numbers. They were voracious consumers of books, magazines, and artistic films. Above all they were passionate fans of rock-and-roll music, which first burst onto the scene in the 1950s. This music, which painted a wild rainbow of color across a largely conservative and sedate suburban landscape, was central to the lives of millions of teens.

By the mid-1960s, rock had become the prime medium of protest and social commentary, reaching nearly every segment of society in nearly every corner of the globe. Bob Dylan, the Beatles, Jimi Hendrix, Cream, Janis Joplin, the Jefferson Airplane, and thousands of other acts filled the air with songs of love, equal rights, introspection, and protest.

Rock and the related sounds of soul music also crossed cultural barriers. In greater numbers than ever before, white teens listened to black singers such as the Supremes and Aretha Franklin as enthusiastically as black teens listened to the Beatles and the Rolling Stones.

A crowd of young people enjoys a rock concert in San Francisco's Golden Gate Park in 1968. During the 1960s, rock music served as a powerful medium of protest and social criticism.

War, Drugs, and Art

Just as the first baby boomers turned eighteen in 1964, the United States became firmly involved in the Vietnam War, which eventually required the military draft of millions of young men. Loud resistance to military action in Southeast Asia was almost immediate on campuses across the country. As the war continued, student demonstrations spilled over to large-scale street protest, and American youth represented a powerful political bloc that was for the first time distinguished mainly by age, as opposed to race or class. This was arguably the first time in history that millions of people seriously challenged their government's authority to wage war.

Added to this volatile mix was the unprecedented, widespread availability of drugs: In the 1960s many millions of Americans were first exposed to psychedelic, or mind-altering, drugs such as peyote, marijuana, mescaline, and LSD (lysergic acid diethylamide—also known as "acid") for recreational use. By the end of the sixties, nearly 6 million baby boomers from junior high school students to rock stars had taken LSD, and up to 20 million—more than one in four baby boomers—had smoked marijuana, or pot.

The hallucinogenic drug experience profoundly influenced fashion, music, art, theater, and film. By the late sixties, in cities throughout the United States, people entertained themselves by decorating their bodies with Day-Glo paint, watching protoplasmic light shows, and dancing all night to so-called psychedelic rock bands. Suburban teens grew long hair, put on love beads and tie-dyed T-shirts, took drugs, and began to seriously question their parents' materialistic values. Hippie culture instead embraced utopian ideals, free love, peace, and the message of mistrust of anyone over thirty.

The art and entertainment of the 1960s continued to influence American culture long after the hippie era had faded and the protest movements had achieved their aims, waned, or refocused their energies. Today, nearly every city in the United States has at least one radio station devoted to music from that era. Albums from sixties bands remain top-selling CDs for record companies, and touring bands such as the Rolling Stones continue to fill stadiums throughout the world. Sixties movies and television series, now viewed as classic, are staples on cable TV. And the literature of the 1960s holds a firm place in modern high school and college literature curricula.

While free speech and freedom of expression have always been cherished American principles, the creative community in the 1960s explored the outer boundaries of those ideals. In doing so, the work often pushed people to look at the unpleasant truths and hypocrisy of modern society and its institutions. Today, it is not unusual for painters, musicians, authors, and other artists to use scathing social commentary to make a point. And in this way, athough the sixties are long gone, the revolutionary spirit of its art and entertainment endures.

A Revolution in Music

Perhaps nothing embodies the spirit of the 1960s better than the music of that era. As the actions of the civil rights, antiwar, and counterculture movements made headlines, the dreams and aspirations promoted by these movements were woven into the lyrics of songs. And as best-selling records promoted peace, love, and equality, these ideals were embraced by people far from the protests and marches that inspired the music. By the end of the decade, rock music had become the prime medium of protest and social commentary, reaching almost every segment of society in nearly every corner of the globe.

Rock music was rebellious from the very beginning. It first burst onto the scene in the mid-1950s when Elvis Presley, Little

Richard, Chuck Berry, Buddy Holly, and Jerry Lee Lewis had a string of number-one hits. Their songs, with lyrics about loving, hugging, kissing, and rocking and rolling, delighted teens as much as they upset parents. In this segregated era, some commentators were appalled that white teenagers were dancing to songs by black musicians. Others were upset by the sexually suggestive lyrics, flamboyant outfits, and outrageous stage manners of artists like Little Richard and Jerry Lee Lewis. Although this was a decade before the civil rights and "free love" movements, early rock musically foreshadowed what was to come.

A series of events, both planned and accidental, brought a sudden end to the fifties-style rebellion. By 1960, Elvis had been drafted into the army and Little Richard had found religion and quit the entertainment business to preach the gospel. Chuck Berry was in prison for transporting a fourteen-year-old girl across state lines for immoral purposes, and Jerry Lee Lewis had been hounded out of the business after he married his fourteen-year-old second cousin. Most tragically, the promising singer Buddy Holly was killed when his airplane crashed

Buddy Holly was part of a group of musicians that introduced Americans to rock and roll in the 1950s.

into an Iowa cornfield. As the new decade dawned, the founding voices of rock had been silenced.

From this void a new breed of stars emerged. They were clean-cut white teenage crooners such as Pat Boone, Fabian, Frankie Avalon, and Paul Anka. Their sugary sweet sounds had so sanitized rock that, in 1962, Bing Crosby, one of the most popular singers from the World War II generation claimed: "Rock 'n' Roll seems to have run its course . . . [and will be replaced by] slow, pretty ballads." [1]

Singing Songs of Protest

Crosby was partially correct. Some 1960s musical trends were anything but calls for revolution. Cheerful melodies and lyrics celebrating sun, surf, and teenage fun characterized the West Coast sound popularized by the Beach Boys and Jan and Dean, and slow, pretty ballads were providing a less edgy contrast to fifties rockers. More and more, however, words to pop songs were political and critical of the status quo. In fact, the ballads soon earned the name "protest songs," and they were based on two musical styles, blues and country, that had been criticizing society for decades.

Since the late nineteenth century, blues songs, written by poor African Americans, had taken as their subject matter the appalling prejudice, discrimination, and poverty under which most black people survived. The lyrics gave musical expression to broken hearts, loneliness, homelessness, and intolerance.

The same was true of songs from the isolated hills of the American South, where rural white musicians composed lyrics about tragedies such as mining disasters, railroad accidents, unfaithful mates, and murders. By the early 1960s, a new generation of musicians were picking up guitars, banjos, mandolins, and fiddles in order to play this music from decades past. Although the singers were mostly white, middle-class teenagers, they wholeheartedly embraced the political values expressed in blues and country ballads. As cultural historians Jane and Michael Stern write, folk musicians "maintained a fundamental belief that honest songs had the power to cut through commercialism, hypocrisy, injustice, inequality, war, and man's inhumanity to man. The music was of hope in [veil] of wrongs."[2]

The folk revival was centered not in farm fields or prison yards, but beneath the skyscrapers of New York City. There, in Greenwich Village coffeehouses and clubs an army of guitar- and banjo-wielding young people gathered to play obscure whaling ballads, chain-gang laments, and other folk music. Many of these singers patterned themselves after Woody Guthrie, who had written dozens of protest songs in the 1930s and 1940s detailing the trials and tribulations of the poor during the Depression. Pete Seeger songs were also popular. These songs, however, were from a different generation as David Hajdu explains in *Positively 4th Street:*

[In 1962, a] million Americans were now purchasing guitars every year, and

Many folk musicians of the 1960s found inspiration in Woody Guthrie's songs of protest.

they all seemed to be sitting in blue jeans and no shoes, strumming "Where Have All the Flowers Gone" and "This Land Is Your Land." There was a breach between the singers and the songs, though. All those idealistic students were young, in their late teens or early twenties. . . .

Most of the songs of idealism they were singing, however timely, were written by members of their parents' generation: "Where Have All the Flowers Gone," by Pete Seeger, whose hair was going gray; "This Land Is Your Land" by Woody Guthrie, who was dying [in a hospital of Huntington's chorea]. More to the point, something about the songs was old-fashioned—not simply old, as all folk music is supposed to sound, but out of fashion—for a generation that grew up on rock and roll. Perhaps it was the singsong quality of the melodies, with their suggestions of children's music and summer camp; or maybe it was the wry puns of the lyrics, which wink in the direction of revolutionary ideas but seem afraid to speak them, let alone scream them out. . . . They were songs that had never seen Elvis on TV.[3]

"People Shouldn't Turn Their Backs"

Bob Dylan was a folksinger who had seen Elvis on television and who had played Presley's songs in a band while growing up in Hibbing, Minnesota. After Dylan moved to Greenwich Village in the early sixties, he shocked many traditional folksingers when he began to sing songs he had written himself. Dylan was a prolific writer, hammering out lyrics to as many as five songs a day on his typewriter. Some of his songs were taken straight from headlines of the day. For example, four songs on Dylan's second album, *Freewheelin'*, were laments against nuclear testing and war. One of them, "A Hard Rain's a-Gonna Fall," was intricate, wordy, and evoked surrealistic, and sometimes harsh, poetic images never before heard in popular music.

Unlike other songs of the day that followed rhythmic formulas, "Hard Rain" was

Pete Seeger (pictured) wrote "Where Have All the Flowers Gone" and other songs popular with folksingers of the early 1960s.

sixty lines and almost seven minutes long. This was highly unusual at a time when radio stations refused to play songs that were much over three minutes long and when almost all popular songs dealt with teenage heartbreak, dating, and love. When asked to comment about his unique protest songs Dylan said: "There's other things in the world besides love and sex that's important too. People shouldn't turn their backs on 'em just because they ain't pretty to look at.

How is the world ever gonna get any better if we're afraid to look at these things?"[4]

Freewheelin' also contained "Blowin' in the Wind," a deceptively simple ballad asking when freedom for all and an end to war will finally come. In Dylan's lyrics, answers to these questions are "blowin' in the wind," but his song was nevertheless a call to action in the face of injustice. Dylan told friends why he wrote "Blowin' in the Wind":

> The idea came to me that you were betrayed by your silence. . . . That all of us in America who didn't speak out were betrayed by our silence. Betrayed by the silence of the people in power. And the others [average Americans] . . . they don't understand. They don't know. They don't even care, that's the worst of it.[5]

Dylan's next album, *The Times They Are A-Changin'* (1964), was filled with protest songs written and performed in a style all his own—his words tumbled out, chanted more than sung, full of colorful allusions and political argument, inventive and passionate. The title track warned parents and politicians that America's children were beyond their command and that a cultural battle was about to shake the nation's windows and rattle its walls. Dylan was branded a genius by critics who called him the voice of the new generation, many of whom set out to look, sound, and think the same way.

Ironically, as his fame increased and a legion of imitators stepped forward to write

protest songs, Bob Dylan moved on to other things. In fact, Dylan wanted to distance himself from any controversy. Arguing that President John Kennedy had been assassinated for his beliefs, Dylan said:

> All I can say is politics is not my thing at all. . . . I can't see myself on a platform talking about how to help people. Because I would get myself killed

Bob Dylan's early songs are characterized by the depth and social relevance of their lyrics.

if I really tried to help anybody. I mean, if somebody really had something to say to help somebody out, just bluntly say the truth, well obviously they're going to be done away with. They're going to be killed.[6]

The Music of Equality

Dylan had some reason to fear those who might wish to silence him for his political messages. In the early years of the sixties, dozens of African Americans who were demanding equal rights in the South were killed by racists, along with several white college students who had joined in their quest to register voters and end segregation. As these current events made headlines, the messages championed in folk songs took on a new urgency as the Sterns write:

The struggle for desegregation in the South in the early sixties—in schools, at lunch counters, at the voting booth—electrified the folk scene. Suddenly those who sang songs of freedom and justice had something that had been conspicuously missing: an urgent issue that was all about freedom and justice. It no longer made sense to revel in America's grass-roots glories when southern blacks were getting chewed by police dogs and beaten by angry mobs. Old slave songs and blues that were the bedrock of the folk repertoire suddenly took on new meaning. Now there were real current-events principles to champion, living evil villains to decry, and . . . energy which yearned to make the world a better place. . . .

As so many of the folkniks joined the protest marches, went south, and experienced oppression firsthand, arm in arm with black brothers and sisters, the meaning of the music changed. . . . Urban white kids wrote home not only about their high-minded mission but about the body odor that arises when one toils all day in the Mississippi sun without benefit of air conditioning; about the chigger bites and rickety cots in bug-infested cabins. For the first time, many folkniks were face to face with the real stuff of which the blues are made.[7]

Folk songs and spirituals took center stage at the March on Washington in August 1963. In the hours before Dr. Martin Luther King Jr. gave his famous "I have a dream" speech, two hundred thousand demonstrators led by popular folksinger Joan Baez sang "We Shall Overcome" and "We Shall Not Be Moved." Folk group Peter, Paul & Mary performed Dylan's "Blowin' in the Wind," which became an instant anthem of the civil rights movement and soon soared to number one on the charts even before most Americans had heard of Dylan.

The following year, during the so-called freedom summer, of 1964, civil rights groups spread out throughout the South to register black voters. Folksingers such as Judy Collins, Phil Ochs, Barbara Dane, and Peter La Farge organized the Mississippi

Joan Baez Leads a Movement

Joan Baez was the first folksinger to achieve international fame. By 1965 she was as well known for her political views as she was for her superb soprano. Baez was the daughter of a Scotch Irish mother and a Mexican father. Growing up in the 1950s, she faced discrimination from an early age because of her deep bronze complexion. In the late 1950s, Baez became a major attraction in the coffeehouses around Harvard University, and in 1959, she received widespread accolades in the national press after her debut performance at the Newport Folk Festival in Rhode Island. By 1962, Baez was selling millions of records and became the first folksinger to appear on the cover of *Time* magazine. She was also instrumental in introducing the world to Bob Dylan, who joined her onstage at Newport, Carnegie Hall, and elsewhere.

Although she could have coasted on her fame and fortune, Baez was intensely political. In 1963, she faced hostile racists and heavily armed police when she marched for desegregation at a protest organized by Martin Luther King Jr. in Birmingham, Alabama. Later that year she appeared at the March on Washington.

In 1966, after the United States became involved in the Vietnam War, Baez sent a letter to the Internal Revenue Service (IRS) informing them that she would not pay her income tax because 60 percent of the money went to the Defense Department. After Baez wrote the letter—and released a copy to the press—she was visited by an IRS agent who warned her that she could go to prison for refusing to pay taxes. Instead the IRS put a lien on Baez's house and car and simply confiscated the cash proceeds from her concerts, adding penalties and fines to the amount legally owed by the singer.

Joan Baez (pictured) was well-known for her social activism as well as her music.

Caravan of Music to sing at voter registration events and equal rights demonstrations.

The British Invasion

Folk musicians struggled to remain true to their political beliefs. The commercial viability of their music, however, was short-circuited nearly overnight when a slew of British bands landed on American shores. This "British invasion," led by the Beatles, also included groups such as the Rolling Stones, the Animals, the Kinks, and countless others. While these groups wrote many of their own songs, they also covered songs by African American artists such as Little Richard, Chuck Berry, Bo Diddly, and Muddy Waters. Although Elvis and many other white pop stars had recorded black American music, the soulful vocals of groups such as the Beatles were truer to the originals, and singer John Lennon publicly acknowledged the band's debt to black recording artists. In this manner, it was said that the Beatles reintroduced black rock and roll to Americans who had forgotten or ignored the African American origins of the world's most popular music.

When the Beatles performed on TV on the *Ed Sullivan Show* on February 9, 1964, more than 73 million Americans—almost

The Beatles found a very receptive audience in America's youth. As the band matured and their lyrics grew more politically charged, the Beatles established themselves as cultural icons.

half the country—tuned in. The Beatles quickly became the hottest band in history, generating a hysteria known as Beatlemania. By April 1964, the five best-selling records on the Billboard charts were Beatles songs, and the group had fourteen singles in the Top 100—records that remain unbroken. For the next several years, the group was at the center of a nonstop whirlwind of concerts, press conferences, TV appearances, and media frenzy.

The Beatles embodied the spirit of the 1960s by continuing to reinvent their music, forging a dynamic blend of sweet acoustic guitars, jangling electric guitars, and lilting bass lines that were unique in pop music. And, like their audience, their lyrics became increasingly political and increasingly experimental. As good-humored ballads gave way to provocative, sophisticated wordplay and darker themes, their songwriting talent and personal charisma made the group cultural icons.

Motown's Soul of the Sixties

While the Beatles changed the very sound of rock music, their only competition was provided by soul singers such as Smokey Robinson, the Supremes, Martha and the Vandellas, Stevie Wonder, the Temptations, Marvin Gaye, Wilson Pickett, and many others.

Soul music was modernized rhythm and blues combined with strains of gospel music that made listeners want to snap their fingers, tap their feet, and dance. The songs revolved around catchy lyrics, tasteful saxophone riffs, and an impeccable rhythm section composed of jangling pianos; crisp, staccato guitar chords; bouncing bass; chiming tambourine; and heavy drums.

Acts such as the Temptations, the Four Tops, and others featured lead vocalists whose tones dripped with a honeyed sweetness. Others, such as James Brown, Aretha Franklin, and Ray Charles, sounded more like gospel singers who belted out soulful melodies guaranteed to command respect. And the importance of sixties soul went beyond just the music. Some of the soul groups, such as the Supremes, were nearly as big as the Beatles, representing the first time that black artists had gained such widespread acceptance among white audiences. Soul's rise came at a time when race relations in the United States were undergoing long-overdue changes.

At the center of the soul revolution was Berry Gordy, a former Ford auto worker, who started Motown Records in a small bungalow on West Grand Boulevard in Detroit. Marked only by a sign that read "HITSVILLE, U.S.A.," this unassuming home was ground zero for the Motown musical explosion that dominated the pop charts throughout the 1960s.

Gordy called Motown's music "the sound of young America." Between 1964 and 1967, the company produced a string of chart-topping hits including "Baby I Need Your Loving" and "Reach Out I'll Be There," by the Four Tops; "Can I Get a Witness" and "How Sweet It Is to Be Loved by You" by Marvin Gaye; "Heat Wave" and "Nowhere to Run" by Martha and the Vandellas; and the biggest-selling

Aretha Franklin Demands R-E-S-P-E-C-T

The civil rights movement of the early sixties gave a measure of political clout to African Americans for the first time in the twentieth century. As young African Americans flexed their new political muscle, several soul artists released songs such as James Brown's "Say It Loud, I'm Black and I'm Proud" (1969) and Marvin Gaye's "What's Goin' On" (1971), which acted as soundtracks to what came to be called the black power movement. But nothing grabbed the listener like Aretha Franklin spelling out R-E-S-P-E-C-T, in her 1967 hit "Respect," as Gillian G. Gaar writes in She's a Rebel:

"Respect" hit a potent nerve in 1967. . . . Riots broke out in the black neighborhoods of several cities across America throughout the summer. . . . [As Phyl Garland wrote:] "Newspapers, periodicals and television commentators pondered the question of 'Why?' as Aretha Franklin spelled it all out in one word, R-E-S-P-E-C-T!" . . . *Ebony* writer David Llorens dubbed 1967 "the summer of 'Retha, Rap and Revolt!'" But "Respect's" broad appeal was also due to the fact that the song could be read in a number of different ways. "It could be a racial situation, it could be a political situation, it could be just the man-woman situation," Tom Dowd, the recording engineer for the song, told *Rolling Stone,* adding, "Anybody could identify with it. It cut a lot of ground." . . .

"Respect" was followed into the Top 10 by . . . "(You Make Me Feel Like) A Natural Woman" and the LP *Aretha Arrives.* She began 1968 with a smash-hit single and album, "Chain of Fools" . . . and *Lady Soul;* each went to number 2 in the charts. During the rest of '68 and '69 she would have eleven further Top 40 singles, three more Top 20 albums . . . and win the first two in a string of ten consecutive Grammy awards. . . .

By the end of the decade Aretha Franklin was clearly one of America's top female singers and an international star.

hits "You Can't Hurry Love," "Baby Love," and "Stop! In the Name of Love" for the Supremes.

Through his management company, International Talent Management, music mogul Gordy also groomed his stars to play at the best venues in the world, many of which had previously been off-limits to black people. Gordy felt that in order to present his acts to the widest audience, he needed to teach the singers, many of whom grew up poor in Detroit housing projects, how to project an image of elegance and grace. To facilitate this goal, Gordy hired Maxine Powell, who owned a finishing and modeling school, to groom Motown artists. Powell described her work:

The singers were raw. . . . They were from the streets, and like most of us who came out of the [housing] projects, they were a little crude: some were backward, some were arrogant. . . . We were training them for Buckingham Palace and the White House, so I had my work cut out for me. . . . Many of them had abusive tones of voice, so I had to teach them how to speak in a nonthreatening manner. . . . Some were temperamental and moody; I would lecture them about their attitude. . . . We really wanted young blacks to understand that you do not have to look like you came out of the ghetto in order to be somebody other blacks and even whites would respect when you made it big. [8]

Gordy put a refined middle-American gloss on Motown artists during an era in which bloody inner-city riots and the rise of black power made many whites suspicious or even antagonistic toward any manifestation of African American culture. But the music was so good that the seemingly incongruous vision of the Four Tops in tuxedos and the Supremes in ball gowns did not seem out of place in a world of longhaired, tie-dyed hippie fashion.

Folk Gets Stoned

The clean, crisp sounds of Motown stood in stark contrast to other popular music of the day, which was strongly influenced by musicians who were regularly using large quantities of psychedelic drugs. And once again, Bob Dylan was at the forefront of the musical movement.

Many of Dylan's fans, according to Michael Gray in *Song & Dance Man III*, were "students and liberals who considered themselves radicals, hated pop music and wore Dylan on their sleeves like a political armband." [9] These people were aghast when, in 1965, Dylan famously "went electric" with the release of *Bringing It All Back Home*. On this album, Dylan ripped into his songs with a Fender Stratocaster in hand, backed by a jangling rock ensemble.

A year later, Dylan released *Blonde on Blonde*. In the song "Rainy Day Women No. 12 & 35" Dylan sang that everyone must get stoned. This was either one of the first prodrug songs of the sixties or a commentary about the verbal stones hurled by his critics. By that time, according to Hajdu, Dylan "chain-smoked marijuana while he composed his work." [10] The singer also took LSD, amphetamines, and other drugs that profoundly affected his music.

While some of Dylan's folk fans were at first unhappy with this new music, the idea of combining folk-style lyrics with a rock beat quickly caught on. For the next few years, this new style of music, called folk rock, was played by the most popular bands including the Beatles, the Rolling Stones, the Byrds, the Mamas and Papas, and countless others. Some songs by these bands also combined elements of country, blues, jazz, and even 1920s vaudeville. The

The Byrds were the first of several bands that combined folk lyrics with a rock beat to create a new style of music known as folk rock.

influence of drugs quickly turned popular music from simple love songs to an "anything goes" potpourri of sound that permanently reshaped rock and roll.

The Beatles Go Psychedelic

When the Beatles began to use the psychedelic drug LSD in 1966, their music underwent a mind-blowing change. Two of the songs on their 1966 album *Revolver,* "She Said She Said" and "Yellow Submarine," were inspired by LSD trips. Lennon's acid-drenched vocals filled out such expansive songs as "I'm Only Sleeping" and "Tomorrow Never Knows," whose words were based on the Tibetan *Book of the Dead,* an ancient text that holy men read to dying Tibetans to help them on their journey through death and rebirth. No one had ever drawn on such serious philosophical concepts for a rock song before.

Although they still recorded on four-track tape equipment that severely limited what could actually be heard on a record, the Beatles filled in songs with backward guitar licks, distortion, filters, and unconventional musical instruments. They added violins, cellos, trumpets, French horns, and other instruments traditionally used in classical music performance.

In 1967, the Beatles released the album *Sgt. Pepper's Lonely Hearts Club Band,* the first rock "concept" album—one in which all the songs seemed to be joined to one another. The swirling psychedelic sounds on the album instantly became the soundtrack for the 1967 "summer of love."

Instead of using their popularity for self-aggrandizement or to sell commercial products, however, the Beatles seemed to be selling the message of peace and love to a generation hungry for a positive message.

The Hendrix Experience

Jimi Hendrix, born in Seattle in 1942, has often been labeled by critics as arguably the greatest guitarist of the twentieth century.

The left-handed Hendrix, who played his Stratocaster guitar upside down, was unknown in America until 1967 when he played at the Monterey (California) Pop Festival. Dressed in buckles, beads, and feather boas, Hendrix stood in front of the mesmerized crowd playing guitar with his teeth. The wall of Marshall amplifiers behind him shrieked with feedback as he put his fuzz tone, wah-wah, and phase-effect pedals to the test. As the entire stage groaned and vibrated with the convoluted cascade of Hendrix's lead notes during "Wild Thing," the guitarist bent over, soaked his beloved Strat in lighter fluid, and set it on fire. By the time the movie chronicling that performance, *Monterey Pop,* was released later that year, Hendrix was a guitar superstar, and anyone who heard him knew that rock and roll would never be the same.

Hendrix released an incredible three albums in two years: *Are You Experienced?*, *Axis—Bold as Love,* and the double album *Electric Lady Land.* Songs such as "Purple Haze" and his version of the Dylan song "All Along the Watchtower" became instant radio staples. Then, in September 1970, it all came crashing down. A drunken Hendrix accidentally took too many powerful sleeping pills and died just two months short of his twenty-eighth birthday.

Although Hendrix's career was cut short, the fuzz-induced frenzy of his guitar work was imitated by millions of guitar players, and a new genre—heavy metal—grew up directly from his flying fingers. He changed what it meant to be a lead guitarist, and though some would try, few would have the talent or free spirit to match Hendrix's technical or creative virtuosity.

Many people consider Jimi Hendrix (center) the greatest electric guitarist of the twentieth century.

And while they faced heavy criticism for their positions, they continued to produce music that was innovative, fresh, and new.

The San Francisco Sound

By 1967, America was in the midst of a counterculture, or hippie, movement. The epicenter of the social upheaval was the Haight-Ashbury neighborhood in San Francisco, a rundown area where affordable apartments butted up against the pastoral Golden Gate Park. Fueled by marijuana, LSD, hallucinogenic mushrooms, and peyote, several San Francisco bands emerged in Haight-Ashbury in the mid-sixties that made music the *San Francisco Oracle* called "regenerative and revolutionary art, offering us our first real hope for the future." [11]

The sound of acid rock emerged in 1965 when Ken Kesey held a series of "acid tests" in San Francisco. The house band for the acid tests was the Grateful Dead, who fused country, blues, jazz, and bluegrass on electric instruments and formed a new brand of music sometimes called "acid jazz" because it relied on the improvisation and free-form expression found in jazz music.

The Grateful Dead recorded several albums considered by critics to be psychedelic masterpieces including *Anthem of the Sun* and *Aoxomoxoa*. On these records, the band mixed the swirling sounds of acid rock with jazz and folk overtones hoping to achieve the aural equivalent of an LSD trip. At a time when three-minute songs ruled radio, the Dead produced songs filled with screaming guitars, chaotic drums, thundering bass, and cascading organ riffs that lasted more than twenty minutes. While other bands were making millions of dollars with concerts and recordings, the Grateful Dead gave their music away for free. As their road manager Rock Scully explained: "We don't do what the system says—make single hits, play big gigs, do the success number. . . . The summer of '67, when all the other groups were making it, we were playing free in the park, man, trying to cool the Haight-Ashbury." [12]

Liberated Women

The Jefferson Airplane often appeared with the Dead at free concerts in Golden Gate Park. Unlike the Dead, whose trippy lyrics were taken from the psychedelic poetry of lyricist Robert Hunter, the Airplane sang openly of drugs, sex, and revolution. The band was led by Grace Slick, the premier psychedelic rock goddess whose soaring, swooping vibrato vocals placed her center stage as one of the first women ever to front a rock-and-roll band. When the Jefferson Airplane released the album *Surrealistic Pillow* in 1967, music fans across the globe were able to hear the encapsulated San Francisco sound on the song "White Rabbit," based on *Alice in Wonderland*, which, like the story, has references to pills, mushrooms, and dreamlike experiences. When asked about the lyrics to the psychedelic masterpiece "Somebody to Love," Slick said they say: "Be free—free in love, free in sex." Added singer Marty Balin, "We're not about entertaining, we're making love." [13]

Three Days of Peace, Love, and Music

Throughout the second half of the 1960s, rock musicians and the counterculture fed off each other and inspired one another. This synergy culminated at the Woodstock Arts and Crafts Festival in White Lake, New York, in August 1969.

The three-day concert, now known simply as Woodstock, featured twenty-seven popular musical acts such as the Grateful Dead, Janis Joplin, the Who, Santana, Arlo Guthrie, the Jefferson Airplane, Crosby, Stills, Nash & Young, and Jimi Hendrix. While the promoters originally hoped that fifty thousand people would attend the concert, no one was prepared for the nearly half-million people who made their way to Woodstock. There was not enough food, water, or bathrooms for the huge crowds; the New York State Throughway was closed because of the traffic; and severe rainstorms turned the concert site into a quagmire. Despite the hardships, people shared food and clothing and there was little in the way of violence or crime. As the promoters boasted, with hippies running the show, it was simply three days of peace, love, and music.

Nearly five hundred thousand people attended Woodstock's "3 days of peace and music" in 1969.

The promise of what became known as the Woodstock Nation was forever immortalized in the 1970 documentary film *Woodstock*. The movie presents a joyous tribute to the late sixties, a time when millions of people believed that peace, love, and music could change a violent world.

San Francisco's other liberated woman was Texas-born Janis Joplin, who was strongly influenced by the blues. After joining a band called Big Brother and the Holding Company in 1966, Joplin became a star almost overnight. She was famous for wailing out songs such as "Piece of My Heart" and "Ball and Chain" with eyes closed, face contorted with pain, clutching a microphone in one hand and a bottle of Southern Comfort whiskey in the other. She shrieked, moaned, cried, screamed, and pounded her feet, lost in a world of her own while singing to thousands of people.

Like other rock stars who create an outrageous public image for themselves, Joplin became trapped in the role of a rowdy, drunken blues singer, often known as much for her shocking behavior as for her music. To her female fans, however, she symbolized rebellion against traditional feminine roles in an era before women's liberation. As Alice Echols writes in *Scars of Sweet Paradise:*

> Janis's success had a lot to do with timing: she expressed women's anger and disappointment before feminism

Artists like Janis Joplin (left) and Grace Slick (right) rebelled against traditional female roles and inspired their fans to do the same.

legitimized their expression. Her refusal to sound or look pretty prefigured feminism's demolition of good-girl femininity, and much of her music . . . protests women's powerlessness in matters of the heart. [14]

The End of an Era

In many ways the symbol of rock and roll in the 1960s was the 1969 New York music festival known as Woodstock. Loud, out of control, and exuberant, the concert and the documentary film that followed gave the name Woodstock Nation to a generation of young music lovers. Peace, love, and rock and roll soon gave way to more sobering images, however, symbolized by the violence of a 1969 Rolling Stones concert at Altamont, California. The Beatles broke up in April 1970, and the drug-and-alcohol-related deaths of Jimi Hendrix, the Doors lead singer Jim Morrison, and Janis Joplin made 1970 a watershed year for rock music.

The decade had begun with earnest white folk singers trying to attach new importance and meaning to traditional forms of music. In ten short years, several new genres were invented that resonated through the music world for decades to come. The three-chord rock of Chuck Berry and Elvis Presley had been reshaped into sweet soul music, angry songs of protest, surrealistic dreamscapes of sound, and a psychedelic blues fury. The notes played and the words written in that decade changed the world, and they would continue to influence rock musicians well into the twenty-first century.

Art for the Commercial Age

The 1960s produced many strikingly incongruous images: housewives dressed as hippies, soldiers protesting a war, and millionaire rock stars advocating revolution. Contradictory images from the world of art could be added to that list. While psychedelic colors were spread across everything from T-shirts to billboards and automobiles, the most iconic art images from the decade are paintings of Campbell's Soup cans and Brillo Soap Pad boxes. Artists historically have sometimes represented anti-establishment views, but instead of rejecting materialism and convention, some of the artistic avant-garde began to treat art as nothing more than a business. As Andy Warhol, one of the leading artists of the decade, stated: "Making money is art and working is art and good business is the best art. . . . I [want] to be an Art Businessman or Business Artist."[15]

Soup to Art

Warhol was at the forefront of the pop art movement, which considered everyday objects, including soup labels, cigarette packs, and comic strips, to be works of art. Pop (as in "popular") art, was strongly inspired by the imagery and messages of advertising; thus pop artists challenged the distinction between modern art for the masses and the "fine" art traditionally displayed in museums.

Warhol, who was a commercial artist in New York City in 1962, started the pop art trend when a friend suggested that he make a painting of something very common, something everyone would recognize, "like a can of Campbell's soup."[16] A few months later, Warhol displayed thirty-two oversized, realistic paintings of Campbell's Soup cans in a Los Angeles gallery. Some canvases featured a single can, others had one hundred cans of different flavors, such as black bean soup, bean and bacon, and vegetable. Critics panned the show for its trite subject matter, while the gallery next door stacked real cans of Campbell's Soup in the window, offering to sell the "artwork" to collectors for twenty-nine cents. Despite the scorn and negative reviews, the publicity garnered Warhol national media attention and he returned to New York a sensation.

Warhol cultivated his sudden celebrity. He set up an art studio in New York and named it "the Factory." As the name implies, Warhol used the Factory to mass-produce art. Abandoning paintbrushes, Warhol created silk-screen portraits of famous people such as actress Marilyn Monroe, former First Lady Jackie Kennedy, and Chinese dictator Mao Zedong. The silk-screen process involves burning a photographic image onto a framed screen. Ink or paint is poured into the screen and transferred to canvas, cloth, or paper with a squeegee. This process allowed Warhol to make multiple prints or put several of the exact same images on one piece of canvas. Using garish pinks, reds, greens, and yellows, the portraits, according to the Andy Warhol Homepage, "can be taken as comments on the banality, harshness, and ambiguity of American culture."[17]

Meanwhile Warhol's images sold for large sums and replaced classic art in the homes of wealthy art enthusiasts. As collector Leon Kraushar stated: "All that other [art]—it's old, it's old, it's antique. Renoir? I hate him. Cezanne? Bedroom pictures. It's all the same. . . . Pop is the art of today and tomorrow and the future. These pictures are like IBM stock, don't forget that, and this is the time to buy, because Pop is never going to die."[18]

Andy Warhol led the pop art movement that challenged the distinction between modern and fine art.

27

"The Art of Underwear"

Silkscreening allowed Warhol to mass-produce images of supermarket products such as Coke bottles, Brillo Soap Pads, Mott's Apple Juice, and Heinz Tomato Ketchup. In 1964, a Manhattan art gallery took this concept to its logical extreme, displaying an exhibit of Warhol's work alongside real food. The gallery was decorated to look like an A&P grocery store, and Warhol's paintings of soup cans were selling for $1,500 while a real 17-cent soup can autographed by Warhol sold for $6. A hunk of genuine Swiss cheese was priced at $27, while a dozen eggs were

As a filmmaker, Andy Warhol explored the themes of boredom, repetition, and public gullibility.

$144. Whether or not art patrons bought the real food is unknown.

In another act meant to mock the concept of art, Warhol held a "Do-It-Yourself" show in which pictures were half colored, and patrons were given crayons and color pencils and encouraged to finish the work.

Even as Warhol made a fortune and built an industry out of simultaneously mocking and glorifying consumer products and celebrity, advertisers quickly began to capitalize on the trend. Thanks to Andy Warhol, by the last third of the decade, shoppers could purchase inflatable Seven-Up cans and Coke bottles, Alka Seltzer pillows, Heinz Ketchup towels, and even a paper dress adorned with black and yellow images from the Yellow Pages phone book. Pop artist Claes Oldenburg celebrated the banality of selling art as a consumer product, commenting:

> I am for the art of underwear and the art of taxicabs. I am for the art of ice cream cones dropped on concrete. I am for the blinking art, lighting up the night. I am for falling, splashing, wiggling, jumping, going on and off. I am for the art of fat truck-tires and black eyes. I am for Kool Art, 7-up Art, Pepsi Art, Sunkist Art . . . , 39 cents Art and 9.99 Art.[19]

Meanwhile Warhol began using film to explore concepts of boredom, repetition, and, it was suggested, public gullibility. His film *Sleep* shows a man sleeping for eight hours. The first forty-five minutes of the film

The Stark Realism of Diane Arbus

Realism in sixties artwork concerned much more than soup cans and spaghetti. Photographer Diane Arbus used her camera to give art patrons a glimpse into a darker side of life few had seen. Arbus was a photographer in the prestigious New York fashion industry in the late fifties. In the early sixties, she abandoned her glamorous job and began taking hundreds of photos of prostitutes, transvestites, mental patients, nudists, and circus sideshow acts—people she called "freaks." Having grown up in a safe, middle-class environment, Arbus explains, on The Photography of Diane Arbus website, why she took on the role as photographic messenger from the fringe:

> Freaks was a thing I photographed a lot . . . and it had a terrific kind of excitement for me. I just used to adore them. I still do adore some of them. I don't quite mean they're my best friends but they made me feel a mixture of shame and awe. . . . Most people go through life dreading they'll have a traumatic experience. Freaks were born with their trauma. They've already passed their test in life. They're aristocrats.

The stark realism that Arbus captured in her photographs, allowed her to thrive in the exclusive New York art scene, far from the seedy nudist camps, freak shows, and transvestite bars patronized by her subjects. Although the photographer received several prestigious Guggenheim Fellowships throughout the sixties, she suffered from serious depression and suicidal tendencies. Arbus killed herself in July 1971, but her work has inspired countless photographers to erase the line between camera operator and subject and portray sometimes unattractive subjects with a sympathetic, yet unflinching, eye.

shows his buttocks gently rising and falling as he breathes. *Empire* is a single eight-hour shot of the Empire State Building. By the end of the decade, Warhol had made more than three hundred movies with a regular cast of petty criminals and social outcasts he called "superstars." Audiences and critics variously found them mesmerizing, offensive, or stupefyingly boring, and combed them for meaning that Warhol insisted was not there.

By the mid-sixties, Warhol was as famous as any rock star and the Factory attracted all manner of hip, young celebrities, musicians, artists, and models. Heavy drug use, transvestism, free love, and homosexuality were practiced openly. Meanwhile, the style he had made famous had radically changed the art business, which had been struggling throughout the 1950s. Tom Wolfe explains in *Painted Word:*

> Pop Art absolutely rejuvenated the New York art scene. It did for the galleries, the collectors, the gallery-goers, the art-minded press, and the artists' incomes about what the Beatles did for the music business at about the same time. It was a thaw! It was spring again! The press embraced Pop Art with . . . delight . . . money, status . . . and even the 1960s idea of sexiness— it all buzzed around Pop Art. [20]

Pop Art as Political Statement

Warhol's pop art was easily embraced by the public because its message was, at least on the surface, not controversial. Artist James Rosenquist, however, used the popularity of the style to convey antiwar and other messages.

Rosenquist began his career painting gigantic advertising images on billboards in New York's Times Square. He painted signs to advertise movies with portraits of Joanne Woodward fifty-eight feet high. He also painted massive signs with Hebrew National salamis and Franco-American spaghetti. In 1962, finding the work unfulfilling, he decided to quit, rent a studio, and create huge images of pop art. In *The Sixties,* Rosenquist explains his motivations for such work:

> I was a child of the advertising bombardment, and though I hadn't liked the outcome of my work in Times Square, the largeness of it had been a blow on the consciousness. I began to use fragments of realistic images—a huge image of spaghetti, somebody's nose as big as a ski slide with eyes three feet wide. People looking at my pictures could identify the elements *bam bam bam bam,* and the most magnified image, the key to the picture, would hit them at last. [21]

One of Rosenquist's most famous paintings, *F-111,* features an eighty-five-foot-long image of an F-111 fighter jet. The painting is made up of panels two-feet square, which were meant to be sold individually, a commentary on mass production in art. The collagelike painting was also adorned with pictures of everyday objects such as a hair dryer, spilled spaghetti, and a light bulb that were meant to show the trivial products of the affluent modern world in contrast to one of its most deadly machines.

Rosenquist continued to work themes of antiviolence and death into his work. He remained adamantly antiwar and often participated in public protest against the Vietnam War.

Comics As Art

By combining spaghetti and jet fighters, Rosenquist added an element of humor to his work that was a commercial element of pop art. Another former commercial artist, Roy Lichtenstein, took this concept one step further when he created large, brightly colored paintings taken from comic strips.

Roy Lichtenstein (pictured) gained popularity for his paintings inspired by comic strips.

Well, if you can imagine how "shocking" it was to see a comic strip on the wall of [an exclusive New York art] gallery in 1962, it got a lot of attention. [Suddenly Lichtenstein] took what was kind of an illegitimate subject for art and painted it in such a way that when you saw the object . . . on the wall, it said, "I am a serious painting." And people believed it. . . . [That painting] was sold to the architect Philip Johnson, the man famous for sophisticated taste. And Lichtenstein was really very easy to see as a classy and elegant and always sort of twinkly and funny image on the wall. [22]

Lichtenstein's images were an immediate hit with the art-buying public, and the painter continued to lift images from various comics popular at the time including romance, science fiction, and war comics. The painting *Takka Takka* describes the harsh life of a soldier. In black capital letters on a yellow background the top third of the painting states: "THE EXHAUSTED SOLDIERS, SLEEPLESS FOR FIVE AND SIX DAYS AT A TIME, ALWAYS HUNGRY FOR DECENT CHOW, SUFFERING FROM TROPICAL FUNGUS INFECTIONS, KEPT FIGHTING!" [23] Beneath, comic book images of a machine-gun barrel spitting fire and a hand grenade flying are pictured with the words "TAKKA TAKKA," painted in red. This and similar Lichtenstein paintings offered subtle commentaries by portraying destruction and violence in childlike, comic book images, full

Lichtenstein first gained notice with the painting *Look Mickey*, which featured images of Donald Duck and Mickey Mouse. While Mickey Mouse looks at a fishing pier, a wild-eyed Donald Duck shouts to him about the giant fish he thinks he has caught. Donald says, "Look Mickey, I've hooked a big one!!" In fact, the "fish" is Donald's own coattails, which he has unknowingly hooked behind his back. *Washington Post* art critic Paul Richard, explains why this was considered innovative at the time:

Pop Goes Op

In the mid-1960s, op, or optical art, became very popular in the United States and Europe. This style of art is based on optical illusions that trick the eye into thinking that a static image is pulsating, vibrating, or flickering. Artists created op art by painting a repetitive series of parallel lines, checkerboard patterns, or concentric circles. Early op paintings featured black-and-white patterns. In the later part of the decade, influenced by psychedelic experiences, op artists created works with bright, contrasting colors such as orange and blue.

The term *op art* was coined by a *Time* magazine journalist in 1964, who realized it rhymed with pop art, which was growing in popularity at that time. By the end of the decade, designers were incorporating op art into clothing, posters, buttons, bumper stickers, and even shopping bags.

Models show off the latest op-art fashion in 1966.

of primary colors and bold lines. Lichtenstein's canvases appeared to be blowups of actual comic strip panels. He imitated the mass-production printing process down to the oversized dots of color, just as printing presses lay color in rows of tiny dots. These dots, called benday dots, became his trademark—flat, repetitive, and unexpressive. By imitating a common mechanical process, Lichtenstein distinguished himself as a leading artist of the 1960s. By the end of the decade, his paintings were bringing the highest prices that were ever paid for the work of any living artist.

Psychedelic Posters

Many popular images in the sixties were taken from commercial products. Some of the most memorable art from that decade, however, came in the form of posters used to promote commercial events, mainly rock concerts in San Francisco. The posters of the sixties, some of which hang today in museums, once adorned telephone poles, record stores, smoke shops, teenagers' bedrooms, and the walls of college dormitories. This art was strongly influenced by the psychedelic experiences of the artists, such as Wes Wilson, who explained: "When I started doing posters, especially the posters in color . . . I think I selected my colors from my visual experiences with LSD."[24]

San Francisco poster art, linked to the counterculture themes of peace, love, and drugs, was, ironically, modeled on advertising used to promote violent contests— boxing matches. "Boxing-style" posters, which were also used for early rock concerts, pictured a prizefighter or performer at the center. The photo was surrounded by block-letter wording that detailed the time, place, and entertainment to be featured. Mid-sixties artists took this clean, easy-to-read format and blurred it into a new style of art to advertise the concerts of the Grateful Dead, Quicksilver Messenger Service, the Jefferson Airplane, and other bands. Social historian David Szatmary describes the style:

The poster art advertising the gatherings captured on paper the acid-inspired, swirling designs of the light shows [at the acid tests]. Though recycling motifs and the lettering of [late-nineteenth-century] art nouveau artists . . . the posters featured a unique graphic style of thick, distorted letters that melted together

against vibrant, multicolored, pulsating backgrounds, which could only be easily deciphered by members of the hippie tribe. They were crafted by Haight artists such as Wes Wilson, Stanley Mouse . . . , Alton Kelley, Victor Moscoso, Bonnie MacLean, Lee Conklin, and Rick Griffin, who also designed album covers for the Grateful Dead and Big Brother and the Holding Company.[25]

The complicated patterns and bright colors of these posters fit right in with hippie culture. In *High Societies* Sally Tomlinson and Walter Medeiros explain why this "people's" art was so appealing:

The hippies rejected middle-class values, including the nine-to-five job. . . . As a result, many people traveled to Haight-Ashbury on foot and had ample leisure time for "hanging out" and for pouring over posters tacked to telephone poles at eye level. Posters that took time to unravel spoke to hippie values. . . . [Deciphering] the posters required concentration, which dovetailed handily with the state of mind which occurs when high on [marijuana and/or psychedelic substance] in which there is often an intense visual involvement in details.[26]

Concert promoter Chet Helms put it more poetically saying the posters "pictured the sensuality, experimentation, and freedom of hippiedom . . . [and] signaled that the joyless head-long rat-race to the top was supplanted by the joyful, sensuous curves and gyrations of the dance, expanding in all directions."[27]

The art on these posters spoke to young people all over the world and their popularity grew every year. In 1965, posters used to promote a single concert at the Avalon or Fillmore Ballrooms were printed in runs of 300. By 1966, thousands of such posters were being printed every month. In 1967, legendary concert promoter Bill Graham was making a fortune paying artists such as Wes Wilson $100 per design while printing 100,000 to 150,000 posters a week. These were shipped to bookstores and "head shops" all over the world. That same year, the Oakland Museum began acquiring the posters for its permanent collection of art, and the style was credited for influencing artists in New York, London, and Paris. The poster art also helped sell the rock bands. According to Tomlinson and Medeiros, "John Cipollina, guitarist for the Quicksilver Messenger Service, reported that when his band traveled across the country young people who had never heard the band's recordings were drawn to the shows by the posters."[28]

Two of the most renowned San Francisco poster artists were Stanley Mouse and Alton Kelley. These men incorporated designs from

Posters were originally designed to promote concerts, but they became a popular art form.

The Art of Underground Comix

While New York artist Roy Lichtenstein elevated cartoon images to art, artist Robert Crumb turned comic books into a controversial voice of the counterculture. With characters such as Mr. Natural, Fritz the Cat, and the big-foot image of Keep on Truckin', Crumb's creations became international icons of the hippie generation. Associated Press writer Jean H. Lee describes the history of "underground comix" on the SouthcoastToday.com website:

Three decades ago, an ex-greeting card designer named Robert Crumb made copies of his comic artwork and hawked them on Haight Street from a baby carriage.

Zap Comix—and a new genre of "underground comix"—was born. Racy and anarchic, Zap rebelled against the restrictive comics code of the 1950s and feasted off the sex, drugs and rock 'n' roll of the late 1960s.

The world of cartooning was under a strict code that forbade the depiction of sex, drugs and profanity when Crumb slapped out the first issues of Zap on newsprint using an old press in 1968. It was a new form, one filled with the most fantastic illustrations of sex and drugs that generation's cartoonists had seen.

"It was as if Walt Disney had dropped acid," recalls [San Francisco artist] Victor Moscoso. "It made no sense whatsoever but it just knocked everyone out . . . ."

"It was something different. These books changed some people's lives throughout the country," says Gary Arlington, a San Francisco comic book seller. Readers outside San Francisco had inklings about the sex and drugs of San Francisco in the '60s but to see the scene in a comic book was mind-boggling.

old movie posters, cartoon characters, and elsewhere. Tomlinson and Medeiros describe their work:

[The] posters created by Mouse and Kelley . . . are lighthearted images, full of fun-loving . . . humor. . . . Mouse Studios created freewheeling designs, as resistant to the existing standards as

the artists themselves were. . . . Mouse and Kelley's posters are full of child-like wonder and sometimes mischief and stand, perhaps more than the work of others, as totems of identity for the Haight-Ashbury society. . . .

Mouse and Kelley appropriated many . . . images: photographs of San

Francisco's infamous earthquake . . . [a] photograph of silent-movie vamp Gloria Swanson . . . neoclassical sculpture . . . and even a contemporary image published in *Life* magazine. . . . The use of copyrighted characters and the drug-related changes the artists made to some of them—Winnie the Pooh and Smokey the Bear, among others—set a precedent for questioning the authority of "the establishment," a practice the hippies embraced with zeal. [29]

Yoko Ono's Conceptual Art

As the popular art of rock posters and soup cans became big business, another school of art developed that renounced commercialism. Conceptual artists rejected artwork that was created for money, believing art was corrupted when it became a commodity for sale. These artists often rebuffed painting, choosing instead to create work from materials such as photos, maps, videos, sculpture, and found objects—things people have discarded. Conceptual art was also called idea art because the ideas of the artist were considered more important than the materials used to create them. As such, a conceptual artwork might be only words printed on a page or a set of instructions describing how to make a piece of art.

Yoko Ono was one of the most renowned conceptual artists of the decade. Ono, a child of privilege, experienced horrors as a child in Japan at the end of World War II when Tokyo was firebombed and the cities of Hiroshima and Nagasaki were leveled by nuclear bombs. She later became a feminist after taking a negative view of the traditional subservience of Japanese women. In her conceptual artwork of the 1960s, Ono tried to convey the loneliness of a child during war using art, performance, and other concepts.

One of Ono's most notorious works was the 1966 *Cut Piece*. In this early piece of performance art, Ono dressed in a traditional Japanese kimono and sat motionless on a stage. She invited members of the audience to cut away pieces of cloth until, after about forty minutes, she was naked, her face mask-like and unemotional. When explaining the meaning of *Cut Piece*, Ono said she wanted to express the isolation remembered from her childhood. She wanted the participants to "hear the kind of sounds that you hear in silence . . . to feel the environment and tension in people's vibrations . . . the sound of fear and darkness . . . [and] . . . alienation." [30]

Not all of Ono's work was so negative, however. Ono often used conceptual art as a way of evoking positive feelings and affirming the power of imagination. In 1966, Ono held a show, *Unfinished Paintings and Objects*, at the Indica Gallery in London. For this show, the artist used found objects that were either transparent or painted white. These tones were meant to convey peace. For example, *White Chess Set* was a standard chess set, but since the board and all the pieces were white, the game, which symbolizes a battle, could not be played in the traditional manner.

Beatle John Lennon attended this show and participated in one of the art pieces. He climbed a ladder to look at a piece of paper attached to the ceiling. Using a magnifying glass provided by Ono, Lennon read the tiny word "YES" written on the paper. Lennon later said, "I felt relieved. . . . It's a great relief when you get up the ladder and you look through the spyglass and it doesn't say *no* or *[screw] you;* it says 'YES.'" [31]

Other "instruction pieces" in the show encouraged visitor participation, a symbolic way of sharing the art with everyone. For example, *Painting to Hammer a Nail* consisted of a white panel, a hammer, and a jar of nails. A card instructed viewers to pound nails into the panel. *Add Color Painting* was a wood panel, brushes, and paints that invited viewers to add to the work.

Art for Peace

After Lennon attended *Unfinished Paintings and Objects,* he and Ono became inseparable. After their 1969 marriage, Ono used Lennon's considerable fame to generate international media attention—and controversy, using the ideas of conceptual art to campaign for peace. In one famous piece of performance art, Ono and Lennon staged a weeklong *Bed-In for Peace* as part of their honeymoon. This art event is described in *Yes Yoko Ono:*

> In *Bed-In for Peace* . . . [Ono and Lennon] converted the . . . 1960s psychedelic gathering-of-the-tribe, the "Be-In," into a week-long international media event. Signs over the couple's marital bed that read "Hair Peace" and

John Lennon and Yoko Ono set up a conceptual art display in a New York museum. Conceptual artists believed artistic ideas to be more important than the materials used to illustrate them.

"Bed Peace" were clear references to Ono's earlier instruction "pieces," transformed into the global language of the countercultural social movement to end the war in Vietnam. . . . In this way, Ono's [artistic statement] reached an international audience and transformed the [conceptual] event into a broad cultural and political statement.[32]

Ono and Lennon continued their peace promotion using ideas based on conceptual art. Before Christmas 1969, the couple conducted a multimedia campaign with the message, "WAR IS OVER!/IF YOU WANT IT/Happy Christmas from John & Yoko."[33] This message was placed on billboards (with appropriate translations) in Hong Kong, London, Tokyo, New York City, and other cities throughout the world. It was also included in the Lennon song "Happy Xmas (War Is Over)" and distributed on posters, postcards, handbills, newspaper advertisements, and radio ads.

Art If You Want It

Most people did not understand Ono's background in conceptual art, and she and Lennon were sometimes ridiculed for their seemingly simplistic ideas. Like other art of the sixties, however, it is recognized today as original, innovative, and creative. It has also been widely imitated in countless venues.

Art has always been used as a way to convey messages about society in a manner left open to interpretation by the viewer. In the 1960s, where some saw a picture of a Brillo box, others saw a commentary on American consumer culture. While hippies took drugs to look at pulsating psychedelic rock posters, art critics saw messages about freedom, spirituality, and connections to the past.

In a sense, artwork of the sixties sent a message that anyone could be an artist. All one needed to do was incorporate elements of advertising, common images, and ordinary objects into a unique artistic statement. Today the influence of pop, op, psychedelic, and other art has become an ingrained part of modern culture. Once the exclusive realm of painters and sculptors, art today can encompass a wide range of possibilities, in the words of Ono and Lennon, "if you want it."

Chapter 3

The Power of the Written Word

In 1965, the Beatles released a song called "The Word" on the album *Rubber Soul*. Singer-songwriter John Lennon told listeners that the word—in this case, *love*—could set them free. While this lyric may sound trite today, during the 1960s it became an anthem. "The word" came to mean any number of simple messages that possibly offered answers to life's deep philosophical questions. As Philip D. Beidler writes in *Scriptures for a Generation: What We Were Reading in the 1960s*, books that contained "the word" were widely discussed on college campuses,

in classrooms, lecture halls, dormitories, apartments, cafeterias, and snack bars; on the quad, the library steps, the union plaza, out on the street, and along every student strip in every college town; in the doorways of bookstores, bars, record [stores], coffeehouses, and head shops; and in progressive . . . curricula . . . and revolutionary student unions and discussion circles. Here was . . . a nation within the nation . . . looking for the Word.[34]

Even as television dominated the lives of most Americans, the printed word was at the forefront of social change. In middle schools, high schools, and on college campuses, books, especially novels, tackled critical issues such as politics, poverty, Eastern religion, injustice, sexism, racism, and war, stirring people's conscience as they engaged the imagination. With almost no advertising by publishers, books such as Kurt Vonnegut's *Cat's Cradle* and Joseph Heller's *Catch-22* became overnight bestsellers by word of mouth alone. The printed word was expected to provide insight as to why African Americans in the world's richest nation were forced to live in grinding poverty. When despair arose over the war in Vietnam, the word focused frustration and outrage into calls for action. And the word was found not only in fiction but also in autobiography, science fiction, humor, and nonfiction.

Confronting Racism

The word in the sixties came from an increasingly diverse segment of society. In previous decades most best-sellers were written by educated white authors. With a few exceptions, the painful stories about the racism and poverty faced by African Americans were rarely mentioned in the pages of popular books. As the civil rights movement gained ground in the early 1960s, however, this began to change.

In cities across the South, black students led a movement demanding an end to segregation at lunch counters, on public transportation, and elsewhere. At the same time, white southern author Harper Lee wrote *To Kill a Mockingbird,* a fictional story based on the reality of life in a small town in Alabama. Published in 1960, Lee's novel is told from the viewpoint of a young girl nicknamed Scout who, wise beyond her years, describes the racism and prejudice around her. Lee won a Pulitzer Prize for

her story in 1961, and the book became a classic.

By the mid-sixties, even as Dr. Martin Luther King Jr. led nonviolent civil rights protests across the South, African Americans in big cities grew increasingly angry and intolerant of white racism. Many found inspiration in *The Autobiography of Malcolm X,* written by Nation of Islam leader Malcolm X. Within the pages of his book, the author described the fear, violence, and pain of racism as no one had done before. The book opens with a chapter called "Nightmare" in

Harper Lee's novel To Kill a Mockingbird *explores the injustice of racism.*

Although many black civil rights activists subscribed to Martin Luther King Jr's (left) philosophy of nonviolence, others embraced the more militant ideas of Malcolm X (right).

which Malcolm imagines himself in his mother's womb in Omaha, Nebraska. Recounting true events, the author describes his mother's intense fear as gun-toting members of the Ku Klux Klan invade her house in search of her husband, a Baptist minister who fought for equal rights.

Racial violence remains a theme throughout the book as the author recalls how his father and four of his uncles died by the hands of white men. The author goes on to describe his move to New York City, his life as a street hustler, and his conversion to the Black Muslim faith while serving time in prison for burglary. The pages seethe with anger as the author refers to white people as "devils" and even criticizes black people who believed in nonviolent change.

The Autobiography of Malcolm X made its author one of most well-known black activists in America, second only to King. Widely quoted in the media, Malcolm argued that black people had been told that they were inferior to whites for so long that they believed it themselves. To counter this, he preached black superiority and pride. As opposed to King, Malcolm believed in violence when confronted with racism, stating that bloodshed was a necessary by-product of any revolution.

Malcolm X was assassinated by a fellow Black Muslim in 1965. His autobiography and other writings, however, have been credited with starting the black power movement that swept the nation in the second half of the 1960s. As Sudhi Rajiv writes in *Forms of Black Consciousness*, Malcolm X pushed the nonviolent integration beliefs of King "into the background [and] also stirred the revolutionary consciousness of his people."[35] The book was also widely read by white people, especially college students. The author's words helped people from the suburbs understand the harsh realities of black life. The book also provided a philosophical basis for the more violent actions of radical white antiwar protesters at the decade's end.

Black Revolutionaries

The Autobiography of Malcolm X was the first of several sixties books written by what Beidler calls the "criminal-intellectual-revolutionary." [36] In 1968, Eldridge Cleaver picked up where Malcolm X had left off when *Soul on Ice* was published by a major New York publishing company.

Soul on Ice is composed of a series of powerful essays Cleaver wrote in prison that were originally published in the left-leaning *Ramparts* magazine. By the time *Soul on Ice* was released, Cleaver was a free man. But he had spent most of his life in prison, first for marijuana possession, then for rape, and then assault with intent to murder. He stated that he was "educated in the Negro ghetto of Los Angeles and at the California state prisons of San Quentin, Folsom, and Soledad." [37]

Like Malcolm X, who also began writing in prison, Cleaver did little to hide his contempt for the racism rampant in twentieth-century America. Radicalized by the riots in urban areas across America, Cleaver promised that black people would have their freedom or "the earth will be leveled by our attempts to gain it." [38] Such ideas quickly became the philosophical foundation for the black power movement.

The ideas in *Soul on Ice* were also championed by radical whites, hippies, antiwar protesters, and others who criticized American capitalism. The following excerpt expresses their alienation and polarization:

It's no secret that in America the blacks are in total rebellion against the System. They want to get their nuts out of the sand. They don't like the way America is run, from top to bottom. In America, everything is owned. Everything is held as private property. Someone has a brand on everything. There is nothing left over. Until recently, the blacks themselves were counted as part of somebody's private property, along with the chickens and goats. The blacks have not forgotten this, principally because they are still treated as if they are part of someone's inventory of assets—or perhaps, in this day of rage against the costs of welfare, blacks are listed among the nation's liabilities. On any account, however, blacks are in no position to respect or help maintain the institution of private property. What they want is to figure out a way to get some of that property for themselves, to divert it to their own needs. This is what it is all about, and this is the real brutality involved. This is the source of all brutality. [39]

While *Soul on Ice* reached number one on the *New York Times* best-seller list, Cleaver was criticized for his inflammatory position and suspected of provoking violence. When he was asked to speak at the University of California at Berkeley, then-governor Ronald Reagan was outraged, saying, "If Eldridge Cleaver is allowed to teach our children, they may come home one night and slit our throats."[40]

Despite such criticism, Cleaver used his notoriety in an unsuccessful run for president on the Peace and Freedom ticket in 1968. He also helped found the Black Panther Party that year and became its information minister, or spokesman. After being wounded in

Protecting Those in Power

During the riots of the 1960s, inner-city neighborhoods in the United States began to look like villages in Vietnam. Both were patrolled by armed men using machine guns, jeeps, and tanks. In the following excerpt from Soul on Ice *author Eldridge Cleaver compares big-city police forces to military units:*

The police do on the domestic level what the armed forces do on the international level: protect the way of life of those in power. The police patrol the city, cordon off communities, blockade neighborhoods, invade homes, search for [guns, drugs, and] that which is hidden. The armed forces patrol the world, invade countries and continents, cordon off nations, blockade islands and whole peoples; they will also overturn villages, neighborhoods, enter homes, huts, caves, searching for that which is hidden. The policeman and the soldier will violate your person, smoke you out with various gases. Each will shoot you, beat your head and body with sticks and clubs, with rifle butts,

run you through with bayonets, shoot holes in your flesh, kill you. They each have unlimited firepower. They will use all that is necessary to bring you to your knees. They won't take no for an answer. If you resist their sticks, they draw their guns. If you resist their guns, they call for reinforcements with bigger guns. Eventually they will come in tanks, in jets, in ships. They will not rest until you surrender or are killed. The policeman and the soldier will have the last word.

In his book Soul on Ice, *Eldridge Cleaver likened inner-city police officers to military soldiers.*

a shootout with police in Oakland, Cleaver left the country and lived for a time in Algeria and Cuba. The popularity of *Soul on Ice*, however, showed that in the tumultuous 1960s, unpolished emotional prose could be a provocative political act that urged others into revolutionary action.

Media Manipulation

Few authors understood the shock value of the written word better than Abbie Hoffman. Although he was college educated and raised in a middle-class neighborhood in Massachusetts, Hoffman used satire, ridicule, and outrageous humor to castigate those in power.

Hoffman's 1968 book, *Revolution for the Hell of It*, published under the pseudonym "Free," describes some of the outlandish political theater undertaken by the author. For example, in May 1967, Hoffman and eighteen others, in order to show the greed of American society, entered the New York Stock Exchange and threw handfuls of one and five dollar bills off the balcony above the trading floor. Stock trading halted as dozens of stockbrokers fell over one another to grab at the money. After Hoffman and the others were ejected from the building, the hippies burned money on the street. That evening Hoffman's "street theater" was featured on television news programs across the country.

Once Hoffman realized that he could manipulate the national media using very few people, he told his readers: "Media is free. Use it. Don't pay for it. Don't buy ads. Make news." [41]

To further the cause of his revolution via media manipulation, Hoffman and several others founded the Youth International Party, or Yippies! Hoffman describes the anarchic nature of the organization:

> Free is the essence of Yippie! We operated Yippie! on less than $4,000 that we raised at a benefit and that we burned in a month. By the end of March we had no money, never used our bank account, had no meetings, had an office with no lock on the door and typewriters that would be liberated [stolen] hours after they were donated. The non-leaders rarely visited the office, people who dropped in found themselves in a vacuum. They were forced to become leaders and spokesmen. They would answer the phones, distribute the leaflets, posters, stickers, and buttons. Everyone would answer the mail and [a member called] Mitch Yippie would pick up the envelopes and sneak them through the postage meter at the place where he worked (he got caught and fired). [42]

Despite their lack of order or agenda, the Yippies! organized a huge antiwar demonstration at the 1968 Democratic Convention in Chicago. The protest turned into a nationally televised riot, and Hoffman was at the center of the whirlwind.

From antiwar marches on Washington to the Chicago riots, *Revolution for the Hell of It* covers many of the legendary moments of the protest movement of the 1960s. On its final pages, the book becomes a how-to

Police arrest author Abbie Hoffman in Washington, D.C. Hoffman used the written word and the power of mass media to encourage American youth to rebel against authority.

manual as the author educates readers on the best ways to "liberate" food, clothing, shelter, and entertainment.

Revolution for the Hell of It sold 3 million copies and, ironically, made its author as rich as those he railed against. The money did not last long, however; Hoffman was forced to spend most of it fighting various criminal charges, such as conspiracy to cause a riot, leveled at him by authorities. Despite the author's legal troubles, *Revolution for the Hell of It* propelled countless white, middle-

class youth toward rebellion. And the book was widely seen as an instruction manual in media manipulation. It also gave people who lived outside mainstream society a sense of community. As Hoffman writes:

> We are cannibals, cowboys, Indians, witches, warlocks. Weird-looking freaks that crawl out of the cracks in America's nightmare. Very visible and, as everyone knows, straight from the white middle-class suburban life. We are a pain in the ass to America because we

Jerry Rubin's Yippie! Dream

Jerry Rubin founded the Yippies! with Abbie Hoffman, and his best-selling book Do It! *was a companion piece to* Revolution for the Hell of It. *The following excerpt from* Do It! *presents the author's idealistic vision of Yippie! utopia:*

At community meetings all over the land, Bob Dylan [songs] will replace The National Anthem.

There will be no more jails, courts or police.

The White House will become a crash pad for anybody without a place to stay in Washington.

The world will become one big commune with food and housing, everything shared.

All watches and clocks will be destroyed.

Barbers will go to rehabilitation camps where they will grow their hair long.

There will be no such crime as "stealing" because everything will be free.

The Pentagon will be replaced by an LSD experimental farm.

There will be no more schools or churches because the entire world will become one church and school.

People will farm in the morning, make music in afternoon and [have sex] wherever and whenever they want to.

The United States of Amerika will become a tiny Yippie island in a vast sea of Yippieland love.

cannot be explained. . . . We are alienated. . . . Our very existence is disruptive. Long hair and freaky clothes are total information. It is not necessary to say [what] we are opposed to. . . . Everybody already knows. . . . We alienate people. We involve people. Attract—Repel. We play on the generation gap. Parents. . . . They are baffled, confused. . . . We tear through the streets. Kids love it. They understand it on an internal level. We are living TV ads, movies. Yippie! There is no program. Program would make our movement sterile. We are living contradictions. I cannot really explain it. I do not even understand it myself.[43]

Hoffman followed up his best-seller with *Woodstock Nation*, a look at the revolutionary politics of rock and roll as demonstrated at the three-day 1969 Woodstock Arts and Crafts Festival in White Lake, New York. This book was followed by yet another best-seller, *Steal This Book*, that lists hundreds of ways to "rip off" large corporations. As the author states: "*Steal This Book* is . . . a manual of survival in the prison that is Amerika. It preaches jailbreak. It shows you where and exactly how to place the dynamite that will destroy the walls."[44]

The Dark Humor of the New Fiction

Hoffman blatantly attacked America, Americans, and American institutions with a brash style that was hard to ignore. Other best-selling authors, however, were more indirect, couching their messages in darkly humorous fiction. Joseph Heller's novel *Catch-22*, for example, exemplified a certain cynical perspective seen in books and films throughout the decade, and popularized the "antihero," a protagonist who lacks the traditional heroic qualities.

Catch-22 brilliantly portrays the horrors of war and the absurdity of military bureaucracy through the tale of bombardier John Yossarian. Yossarian has been traumatized by the violent death of a crewmate and wants out. Indeed there is a way out, but, in Heller's ingenious plot, there is a catch, Catch-22, which turns the definition of sanity inside out. An airman can request a Section 8 discharge on grounds of insanity. Yossarian does not want to fly dangerous missions in which he might be killed and thinks the war is driving him crazy. That, however, is a sane reaction, which therefore means he must continue to fly. The following excerpt between Yossarian and company physician, Doc Daneeka, about a fellow flier named Orr, explains Catch-22:

> Yossarian looked at [Daneeka] soberly and [said]: "Is Orr crazy?"
>
> "He sure is," Doc Daneeka said.
>
> "Can you ground him?"
>
> "I sure can. But first he has to ask me to. That's part of the rule."
>
> "Then why doesn't he ask you to?"
>
> "Because he's crazy," Doc Daneeka said. "He has to be crazy to keep flying combat missions after all the close calls he's had. Sure, I can ground him. But first he has to ask me to."

Joseph Heller (pictured) illustrated the horrors of war and the absurdity of military bureaucracy.in his novel Catch-22

"That's all he has to do to be grounded?"

"That's all. Let him ask me."

"And then you can ground him?" Yossarian asked.

"No. Then I can't ground him."

"You mean there's a catch?"

"Sure there's a catch," Doc Daneeka replied. "Catch-22. Anyone who wants to get out of combat duty isn't really crazy." [45]

Heller based *Catch-22* on his own experiences flying sixty missions as a bombardier in Corsica during World War II. Although his novel was little noticed when it was published in 1961, it became the leading antiwar novel by the end of the decade, selling 3.5 million copies. As the war in Vietnam—and protests against it—escalated, *Catch-22* provided a basis for those who argued that war was insane and military rules were absurd. Today, the term catch-22 is part of the lexicon, describing any situation in which a desired outcome is impossible to attain because of a set of illogical rules or conditions.

The Cuckoo's Nest

In 1962, another novel was published that used black humor to explore the thin line between sanity and insanity. *One Flew over the Cuckoo's Nest* was written by Ken Kesey while the author worked as a night attendant in a psychiatric hospital in Menlo Park, California, near Palo Alto. Before he took the job, Kesey, who was attending Stanford

University on a creative-writing fellowship, had spent many hours at the hospital volunteering as a paid subject in drug experiments. Government researchers paid Kesey and dozens of other students fifty dollars to take the powerful hallucinogen LSD and report on their experiences. After taking the job as a night attendant, Kesey discovered LSD and mescaline were kept stocked in the medicine cabinet in the psychiatric ward where they were used for research into mental illness.

Kesey often spent the late-night hours on his job, high on LSD, observing the inmates in the ward. He later said: "Before I took drugs . . . I didn't know why the guys in the psycho ward at the VA Hospital were there. I didn't understand them. After I took LSD, suddenly I saw it. I saw it all. I listened to them and watched them, and I saw that what they were saying and doing was not so crazy after all." [46]

The antics of the patients inspired Kesey to write *One Flew over the Cuckoo's Nest*, which quickly became a best-seller. The story revolves around Randall Patrick McMurphy, a minor criminal who gets himself committed to an insane asylum in order to avoid serving hard time in prison. McMurphy, however, gets more than he bargained for. The ward is overseen by Nurse Ratched who controls every aspect of the inmates' lives using humiliation, fear, and, most important, rules. Representing society at large, Ratched is described by Beidler as "a walking manual of procedures, protocols, precedents, and regulations." [47]

Much of *One Flew over the Cuckoo's Nest* concerns the contest, at first comical but

Ken Kesey's One Flew over the Cuckoo's Nest *examines the thin line between sanity and insanity.*

eventually deadly serious, between the nurse and McMurphy. The jailbird takes on the role of revolutionary with a heart of gold, defending the defenseless inmates who are constantly browbeaten and intimidated by the nurse. He spars with Ratched over card games, the right of the inmates to watch the World Series, and the right to simply be left alone. In the end, the nurse wins; McMurphy is given a lobotomy, an operation that removes part of his brain and leaves him in a near-vegetative state. A Native American inmate named Chief Broom, who is the actual narrator of the story, puts McMurphy out

of his misery, smothering him with a pillow. Broom believes that a true revolutionary like McMurphy would rather die than live under the control of another.

Like *Catch-22*, Kesey's book was seen by readers as a symbolic battle between sane individuals and crazy institutions, and ultimately between freedom and oppression. And like *Catch-22*, the meaning of *Cuckoo's Nest* grew in importance as the sixties progressed and millions of others became increasingly alienated from mainstream society and to some degree familiar with LSD experiences. As Beidler writes, "it is virtually impossible to overstate the contribution of *[One Flew over the Cuckoo's Nest]* to 60's legend. . . . That book, for vast numbers of 60s youth . . . became pure gospel."[48] And the author of the book was partially responsible for the widespread use of LSD.

With the success of *One Flew over the Cuckoo's Nest*, Kesey bought a cottage in La Honda, outside Palo Alto, and began giving LSD to writers, artists, musicians, and even members of the Hell's Angels motorcycle club. Determined to "turn on" everyone, beginning in 1965 Kesey held a series of "acid tests" in San Francisco. At these huge parties, LSD, which was legal at the time, was freely offered to thousands of people. When details of the acid tests were publicized by the media, young people from all over flooded into San Francisco's Haight-Ashbury neighborhood. Attracted by the promise of drugs and free love, Haight-Ashbury became the hippie mecca, in part because of the success of Kesey's book.

The Underground Press

With the advent of small, inexpensive printing presses in the 1960s, a group of literate radicals began publishing what were called underground papers. Most of these advocated drugs and free sex and espoused left-wing, antiwar, and antiestablishment opinions. Andrew J. Edelstein explains underground papers in The Pop Sixties:

The underground press, a loose confederation of publications chronicling the counterculture, was created in response to [widespread] mistrust of the so-called establishment newspapers. On their pages, you'd find lots of talk about drugs, revolution, rock, sex, and radical politics. . . . These magazines also had weird layouts (tilted columns or columns that didn't run into each other), and weird typography (brightly colored pages in Hindu patterns). Spelling didn't count, except the four-letter words which were always spelled correctly. "Amerika," "Amerikka," or "Czechago" [Chicago] were favorite misspellings. . . .

    The papers themselves ranged from crude and embarrassing scandal sheets to more respectable publications involved in solid investigative reporting. . . . The more politically-extreme papers printed telephone company credit card numbers of prominent people so that readers could charge phone calls to them, or to the home phones of local narcs [narcotics detectives]. They also printed unusual drug-filled recipes [for cooking with marijuana].

    The Big Four of the underground movement were the *Los Angeles Free Press,* the *Berkeley Barb,* New York's *East Village Other,* and San Francisco's *Oracle.* . . . The *Berkeley Barb* reflected the leftist political culture of the California university town, featuring a radical-political columnist known as the Roving Rat Fink. Across the Bay, San Francsico's *Oracle* used rainbow-colored graphics, reflecting the psychedelic excitement of Haight-Ashbury. Its calendar of events was called the "Trips Page," and it featured a gossip columnist called the Gossiping Guru.

Changing Sexual Roles

In the 1960s, there were several reasons for the loosening of sexual inhibitions, exemplified by the free love movement. The birth control pill had been introduced in the early sixties, and by mid-decade, more than 6 million American women were on the pill. By providing nearly 100 percent protection from pregnancy, the pill freed women, for the first time in history, from the fear of unwanted pregnancy. In this era before AIDS, women were suddenly free to join men in widespread sexual experimentation. This was compounded by a loosening of sexual inhibitions due to drugs. Long-held beliefs about sex were flouted by a generation whose anthems were "free love" and "make love not war."

Meanwhile, traditional gender roles were under fire by women such as Betty Friedan, who published *The Feminine Mystique* in 1963. Friedan was inspired to write the book after she attended the fifteenth reunion of Smith College's class of 1942. Friedan conducted a survey of her classmates and discovered that in spite of their general prosperity and well-adjusted lives, many women were bored, unhappy, and vaguely suffering from what Friedan called, "the problem that has no name."[49] Friedan explained the meaning behind the title of her book:

> The feminine mystique is the name I have given to a way of looking at woman that has become epidemic in America during the last 15 years. Based on old prejudices disguised in new . . . dogmas, it defines woman solely in sexual terms, as man's wife, mother, love object, dishwasher and general server of physical needs, and never in human terms, as a person herself. It glorifies woman's only purpose as the fulfillment of her "femininity" through sexual passivity, loving service of husband and children, and dependence on man for all decisions in the world outside the home: "man's world". . . .
>
> [This] sophisticated mishmash of obsolete prejudices (woman's place is in the home; woman is inferior, child-

like, animal-like, incapable of thought or action or contribution to society) has been built up, since World War II, by psychologists, sociologists, educators, marriage counselors, magazines, advertising, and by a combination of historical coincidences (depression and war, the [atom] bomb, the population explosion, the stepped-up speed of change in the world) and misunderstood needs and frustrations of men and women themselves. The result of the feminine mystique . . . is to stunt the growth of women, robbing them of identity and making them virtually displaced persons in our fantastically growing society. Forcing women to

In The Feminine Mystique, *Betty Friedan (below) attacked traditional ideas about women and gender roles.*

live vicariously through love, husband, children . . . is not only making women sick for lack of a self but making love and marriage, husbands and children and our whole society sick.[50]

The Feminine Mystique struck a chord with millions of women and became an instant best seller. By giving name and substance to their common malaise, the book inspired thousands of women to marry later, obtain college education, and pursue their own careers. Gender discrimination, however, remained widespread throughout the sixties, and women who wanted to become professionals faced many hurdles in the workforce.

Sex and the Single Girl

The stereotypical view of women as mothers and housewives began to change considerably in the mid-1960s. At that time, television, movies, and magazines began promoting the image of the happy-go-lucky single girl with a flip hairstyle, polka-dot stockings, long false eyelashes, and a miniskirt.

The idealized concept of the "perky" unmarried woman became fashionable after the publication of the groundbreaking book *Sex and the Single Girl* by Helen Gurley Brown in 1962. Brown opened the book with these words:

Far from being a creature to be pitied and patronized, the single girl is emerging as the newest glamour girl of our times. . . . When a man thinks of a married woman, no matter how lovely she

is, he must inevitably picture her . . . fixing little children's lunches, or scrubbing them down because they've fallen in a mudhole. . . . When a man thinks of a single woman, he pictures her alone in her apartment, smooth legs sheathed in pink silk Capri pants, lying tantalizingly among dozens of satin cushions, trying to read but not very successfully, for HE is in the room—filling her thoughts, her dreams, her life.[51]

Sex and the Single Girl sold millions of copies and was soon published in twenty-

Helen Gurley Brown's Sex and the Single Girl *popularized an idealized concept of the liberated single woman.*

three countries. After the success of her book, Brown was appointed editor of *Cosmopolitan* magazine. The magazine, simply known as was full of tips, formulas, tricks, and tests to help single women, or "Cosmo Girls," in the world of dating, decorating, and entertaining. *Cosmo* also published well-written features by women authors such as Nora Ephron, Gael Greene, and others. And unlike other magazines at the time that were written for general audiences, *Cosmo* was the first to focus on a well-defined segment of the population—the single working woman. As a result, readership soared and Brown became the spokesperson for the swinging sixties single woman.

Social Upheaval and the Word

The success of certain books and magazines in the 1960s was a result of several coincidences: The highly educated baby boomers were raised to be mass consumers of the written word. Meanwhile, new sexual attitudes, an unpopular war, and the widespread use of psychedelic drugs caused many to become deeply analytical. Millions began to question popular beliefs about religion, patriotism, and sexual roles. Just as cultural upheavals were changing society, authors responded with the word. Inspired by these trends, dozens of instant classics were created in ten short years.

Chapter
4

Stage and Screen

Rule breaking and wild experimentation in the 1960s extended to American drama and film. As never before, frank depictions of the counterculture, drug use, nudity, and sex were presented in mainstream playhouses and movie theaters. However, most theatrical and film producers pursued these themes not for creative reasons, but rather for economic ones. By the late sixties, the theater and film industries were both fighting unprecedented economic forces that were threatening to turn out the stage lights. Sex, drugs, and rock and roll proved to be a reliable way to lure customers back into the theaters.

Television was the driving force behind changes onstage and on the silver screen. In 1967 alone, movie attendance dropped 50 percent after one-third of Americans had purchased color television sets, which were new on the market. And movie attendance had been dropping for years, since black-and-white TVs were first made widely available in the early 1950s.

By the late sixties, on New York's Broadway—the theater capital of the United States—large-scale musicals filled with singing and dancing were failing to attract large crowds as they had in earlier years. As Americans suffered through war, assassinations, riots, and protests, these innocuous musical extravaganzas seemed to be quaint and old-fashioned, more a product of the 1950s. Instead theatergoers were patronizing experimental theaters that put on plays that they felt had something to say, plays with themes of social and cultural significance. Producers on Broadway noticed and found some success pursuing this trend.

Changing Themes on Broadway

In the first half of the sixties, Broadway produced classics such as *The Unsinkable Molly Brown, Bye Bye Birdie, Hello Dolly!*, and *Funny Girl*, blockbuster musical productions aimed at entertaining the largest audience possible. In 1964, however, the surprising popularity of *Fiddler on the Roof* proved that a play could take on a tough subject and still sell tickets. Set at the end of the nineteenth century, *Fiddler on the Roof* tells the story of a philosophical Jewish dairy farmer named Tevye who lives in a small town in Russia where Jews face severe discrimination. Tevye's daughter wants to break tradition and marry a poor tailor whom she loves. Her father, however, had arranged for her to wed a well-to-do butcher. Tevye must then decide between his commitment to old Jewish traditions and his daughter's happiness. This story about persecution, poverty, and faith opened the way for other musicals to deal with serious issues while still entertaining theatergoers.

This was most successfully realized in 1966, when the musical *Cabaret*, a play set in Nazi Germany in 1933, became the toast of Broadway. The story follows a young American writer who falls in love with an American cabaret singer in prewar Berlin. While half of the play consists of brilliant musical numbers that take place on the stage of a cabaret, the story has a dark side that

deals with the social conditions in Germany that led to World War II and the Holocaust.

While *Cabaret* and *Fiddler on the Roof* were successful, Broadway was faltering during the second half of the sixties. New productions failed to catch on with the public, and many musicals opened and closed on the same night, with huge financial losses. Ironically, the counterculture, which seemed to be costing musical theater its audience, actually saved it.

The unlikely savior was the musical *Hair*, which premiered in 1968. *Hair* was the first rock musical; that is, a play based on a rock and roll musical score. Critic John

Actors perform a scene from Hair. *The play premiered in 1968 and introduced a new theatrical genre known as the rock musical.*

Kenrick describes the story of *Hair* on the Musicals101.com website:

> [The play involved] a young . . . man who revels in rock and rebellion until he is drafted into the army. This became the [play's] excuse for an explosion of revolutionary proclamations, profanity, protest and hard rock that shook the musical theatre to its roots. . . . [The songs] "Aquarius" and "Let the Sunshine In" became chart-topping hits, and *Hair*'s hippie sensibility (including a brief ensemble nude scene) packed in audiences for several years. [52]

While *Hair* scandalized some mainstream audiences, it successfully broke the nudity taboo in theatrical production. In 1969, the comedic musical *Oh, Calcutta* took advantage of these new attitudes. The play featured rock music, dancing, full-frontal nudity, and sexually explicit humor and skits written by John Lennon and other luminaries. The success of other rock musicals such as *Jesus Christ Superstar* and *Tommy* proved that the genre started by *Hair* was durable and hugely profitable.

Theater for Everyone

While Broadway took sudden interest in cultural upheavals in American society, the very nature of theater production was changing. In earlier decades, the American theater was an exclusive artistic medium. Actors learned their craft at elite acting schools in New York City, London, or Paris. Producers relied on works by best-selling authors or playwrights with many successful productions on their résumés. As the sixties progressed, however, greater numbers of people expressed the desire to be included in theatrical productions. And as more individuals endeavored to express themselves, several new types of theatrical companies emerged.

With large numbers of baby boomers attending colleges and universities, more of these institutions began offering classes in acting, stagecraft, and playwriting and developed degree programs in drama. College theater troupes regularly produced plays, both popular and experimental, often to sold-out crowds.

Meanwhile, the parents of college students started their own theatrical revolution. As the suburban population continued to grow, the numbers of small community theaters increased. These theater companies were filled with housewives, factory and office workers, and other amateurs who acted, sang, and danced simply for fun.

On a more professional level, hundreds of small theater groups produced experimental plays that were not commercial enough for Broadway. These productions became known as "off Broadway" and then "off-off-Broadway." The members of such productions were often serious actors, directors, and writers, who either wanted to augment their small incomes from mainstream venues or were interested in cutting-edge material.

The most popular theaters outside New York City were the large regional repertory theaters that arose in many medium-sized

During the 1960s, off-Broadway theaters like this one became popular as small theater groups produced plays without enough commercial potential for Broadway.

and large cities across the United States. The first was the Guthrie Theater, founded Minneapolis in 1963. Such repertory theaters produced classic plays by Shakespeare and also time-tested works of modern playwrights such as Oscar Wilde and Eugene O'Neill, rather than experimental works by unknowns. At first, repertory theaters were sponsored with subsidies from wealthy donors and city governments. After the National Endowment for the Arts was established by the federal government in 1965, most repertory theaters received federal funds. This was the first time that theater had been subsidized by the U. S. government since 1939 when the depression-era Federal Theater Project was ended.

Alternative Theater

The growing number of theaters fostered an expanding base of actors, writers, and directors who cared about pressing social issues. People who wanted to produce plays about civil rights, free speech, the counterculture, the antiwar movement, feminism, ecology, gay rights, and other topics formed their own theatrical companies, broadly known as "alternative theater."

This new type of theater was different from others in several important aspects. Traditionally, a playwright worked alone to write a script that actors performed onstage. In alternative theater, the writers and actors worked together to create a script. As Theodore Shank writes in

Theater on Street Corners

In the late 1960s, radical theater companies often performed on street corners in order to get their antiwar, antiestablishment messages to the largest possible audience. This sometimes led to humorous confrontations with police, as performer Michael Brown illustrates in The Radical Theatre Notebook *by Arthur Sainer:*

[We] were performing [a play critical of President Nixon] on a Manhattan street corner. Big crowd. Almost at the end of the play and a cop comes to break us up. Well, we start doing a number on him. One of us had an arm around him and is facing the crowd explaining his position to them, telling them they should really leave because it's the law and he's a nice guy doing his job. Other [members of the theater company] are running around . . . with cardboard guns from the play, acting like nasty cops and saying [everyone should leave] or get busted! Still others are screaming like banshees [saying]: You're a bunch of freaks, how come you want to see a play on the street, go home and watch TV alone, get a haircut, no fun allowed on the street, go home. Well, [the audience was] beautiful! They didn't budge, not one of them, not a muscle moved. . . . The cop must have put in a call before coming over, because suddenly there's flashing red lights from all over, so we gather the props, bid the crowd a formal goodbye, thank them for their militance, remind them to keep up the fight for this kind of thing, and with props dangling . . . robes flying in the breeze, run like hell down 6th Avenue, and just get away around a couple of convenient corners.

American Alternative Theater, words became much less important than actions in this type of theater:

There was a distrust of words because of the end to which they were used by politicians and advertising. It was also recognized that some [experiences] cannot be expressed by words, and it was thought that society, having relied upon words, had tended to cut itself off from its experience. . . .

Painters and sculptors who were beginning to create theatre productions were naturally inclined toward visual means, and other theatre artists experimented with non-verbal sounds, with placing focus upon the performer's body, and with a variety of other non-verbal means. [53]

This distrust of words was the operating theory behind The San Francisco Mime Troupe. This company, founded in 1959, used costumes, masks, and body movements to tell stories, rather than words.

Alternative theater also questioned the very notion of a formal playhouse. These small theaters were often set in storefronts, garages, warehouses, or even parking lots and street corners. Such settings tended to blur the distinction between audience and actors, who might use the entire theater space as their stage, as explained by Shank:

Unlike the commercial theatres, [alternative theaters] are not primarily concerned with entertainment as a product to be sold. Instead, they are anxious to improve the quality of life for themselves and their audiences. . . . The traditional theatrical spaces are economically unfeasible and artistically unsuitable. They are too large and typically are divided into stage and auditorium which dictates a particular performer-spectator relationship unacceptable . . . because the arrangement hinders the development of a community spirit. [54]

Minority Groups Present Their Views

The simpler, new methods for creating and presenting plays encouraged dozens of alternative companies to form in towns and cities across the country. Many specialized in specific social movements and pressing issues of the day. For example, the Free Southern Theater was formed in 1963 by black playwrights Gilbert Moses and John O'Neal in Mississippi at the height of the civil rights struggle. The company produced works that illuminated the racism and discrimination experienced by black people. Similar companies used plays to promote black self-esteem, educate audiences, and preach political messages of equality, integration, and even revolution.

In California, Hispanic theaters such as El Teatro Campesino (The Farmworkers Theater) produced bilingual plays in Spanish and English. Often backed by Mexican-style mariachi music, these plays illustrated the problems faced by poor immigrant communities. Oftentimes audiences were asked to sing and dance with the actors at the climax of a performance, increasing audiences' identification with the performers.

Inspired by the advances of other minorities, actors began to perform in openly gay and lesbian roles for the first time in the 1960s. In New York City in 1965, the Playhouse of the Ridiculous used male actors dressed as women in order to make fun of traditional gender roles. As Shank writes: "As with other minority theatres, [gay] groups helped to develop self-acceptance of their minority status and attempted to make themselves more acceptable to the community at large." [55]

Guerrilla Theater

In the second half of the sixties, members of the antiwar and counterculture movements began to form their own alternative theaters. These groups combined various theatrical elements from circuses, carnivals, magic shows, vaudeville, and minstrel shows in order to create unique productions.

For example the Bread and Puppet Theatre in New York City created huge papier-maché "puppets" up to fifteen feet tall. Actors wearing these costumes performed various choreographed moves while narrators told stories. Musicians added songs and sound effects. Such performances often took place in parks, on sidewalks, or at peace rallies. Oftentimes they were protests against the Vietnam War. For example, the play *A Man Says Goodbye to His Mother* shows a puppet with a gas mask, gun, and toy airplane as he dies after bombing and burning enemy villages. His mother stands to the side and watches. Nearly every city had one such troupe, performing what came to be called street theater or guerrilla theater.

One of the most experimental street theater troupes was the Living Theater,

Actors perform with puppets during a 1965 antiwar rally. These kinds of performances often took place on street corners or sidewalks and came to be known as street or guerrilla theater.

which did away with all theatrical trappings. Performances had no set and no script. The performers wore whatever they wanted and often improvised their characters on a moment's notice. From 1964 to 1968, the forty members of the group traveled throughout Europe like nomads. They journeyed through twelve countries, performing only once or twice before moving on. Living communally, and with very little money, the group sometimes did away with clothing all together and performed nude in the street.

By the end of the decade, such experimental groups had taken a form of entertainment popularized by Broadway and turned it on its head. Theater was now seen by some as a method of individual expression that was meant to shock, enlighten, and sometimes bewilder the audience.

Generation Gap on the Silver Screen

The radical changes that were affecting theater would also sweep through the film industry by the end of the decade. And like everything else in Hollywood, the transformation was bigger, flashier, and involved much larger sums of money.

In the early sixties, however, the movie business was on a course similar to Broadway, producing mostly feel-good entertainment for the largest possible audience. By this time, Hollywood had been producing films for more than forty years. The staple product of the 1950s and early 1960s was the so-called family film, designed to appeal to parents who could bring children

to the movies without worrying about hearing profanity or seeing sex and violence. The executives who were in charge of producing these films were, for the most part, the men who had invented the film industry, conservative and now-aging businessmen. For example, Adolph Zukor, the boss at Paramount Studios, was ninety-two years old in 1960. His second in command, Barney Balaban, was seventy-eight. These men had made movies in the thirties during the depression, in the forties during World War II, and in the 1950s.

With power concentrated in the hands of men like these, it was impossible during most of the sixties to make movies that glorified sex and drugs or criticized U.S. policy in Vietnam. This created financial problems for the big studios, however, as Peter Biskind writes in *Easy Riders, Raging Bulls*: "The old men who ran the studios were increasingly out of touch with the vast baby boom audience that was coming of age in the '60s, an audience that was rapidly becoming radicalized and disaffected from its elders."[56]

This generation gap in Hollywood was obvious on the silver screen. Family fare included expensive musicals such as *My Fair Lady* and *The Sound of Music*, aimed at an adult audience, and wholesome, "fun in the sun" beach movies featuring Southern California surf and sand, aimed at teenagers.

The surf movies tended to be formulaic and featured a limited number of look-alike, bankable stars. For example, between 1963 and 1965, teen idol Frankie Avalon starred in *Operation Bikini, Beach Party,*

Annette Funicello and Frankie Avalon starred together in several formulaic surf movies during the 1960s.

Muscle Beach Party, Beach Blanket Bingo, How to Stuff a Wild Bikini, and a spy spoof, *Dr. Goldfoot and the Bikini Machine.* In each movie, Avalon pursued the buxom former *Mickey Mouse Club* Mouseketeer Annette Funicello as various ridiculous villains tried to stop him. As Andrew J. Edelstein writes in *The Pop Sixties,* the movies "featured an ensemble cast of morons adrift in a self-contained world of sand, sea, and palm trees." [57]

Then, in June 1964, the focus suddenly shifted from Southern California to England as the Beatles burst onto the screen with *A Hard Day's Night.* It was released only four months after the group appeared on television on the *Ed Sullivan Show,* and Beatlemania was sweeping the country.

Just about every American teenager saw *A Hard Day's Night.* It opened in five hundred American movie theaters and grossed $1.3 million in its first week, a huge sum at the time. More than a commercial success, the movie certified the Beatles as bona fide movie stars and enhanced their status as charming, irreverent heroes of the young generation. In an innovative blend of reality and fantasy, the Beatles played themselves playing rock stars with wit and style. The shots of the Beatles traveling, hanging around backstage, and answering fan mail in hotel rooms also humanized the four band members and endeared them to their fans.

A Hard Day's Night was the first true music video ever filmed, with "jump cuts" of the band leaping through the air, running wildly across empty fields, playing live concerts before screaming audiences, and being chased through London's streets by teenage girls. The technique, which has been imitated endlessly on MTV music videos, helped make the movie a classic. Even in the twenty-first century, movie critic Roger Ebert uses *A Hard Day's Night* to teach film classes, analyzing it with his students one shot at a time.

Major Changes in Hollywood

Despite the success of *A Hard Day's Night,* and a second Beatles movie *Help!,* the movie industry continued to flounder. As society underwent wrenching transformation, the studios continued to bet huge sums of money on bigger and bigger pictures. Many based merely on spectacle flopped.

As many big studios threatened to close their doors, the void was filled by a new breed of creative, young filmmakers who were not afraid to make controversial movies. Like the Beatles, this movement came from Europe. In 1967, Italian director Michelangelo Antonioni shocked audiences when he showed full frontal female nudity in *Blowup*. That same year, British director John Boorman made *Point Blank*, an art film about greed and betrayal that featured some of the most graphic violence ever seen at that time. While these films offended conservative movie executives, the studios could not ignore the large sums of money these cheaply produced films were pulling in.

In Hollywood, success breeds imitation, and soon big studios were ordering pictures featuring more graphic scenes of sex and violence. The first was *Bonnie and Clyde*, the story of small-time, depression-era bank robbers. At the end of the film Bonnie and Clyde die in a hail of machine-gun fire filmed in slow motion, one of the bloodiest scenes ever shown up to that time. The film's popularity has been explained in part by the fact that although the film was set in the 1930s, it had a noticeably 1960s viewpoint, as Seth Cagin and Philip Dray write in *Born to Be Wild*:

> Bonnie and Clyde . . . were distinctly modern heroes, familiar figures to a

Bonnie and Clyde, a film about the infamous depression-era gangsters, was the first Hollywood movie with scenes of graphic violence and sex.

The Dark Humor of *Dr. Strangelove*

The first popular movie to mock the president of the United States, his advisers, and the U.S. military was written and directed by American-born filmmaker Stanley Kubrick, who worked in Britain for most of his career. Released in 1964, Dr. Strangelove; or, How I Learned to Stop Worrying and Love the Bomb *used black humor and slapstick to tell the story of the world ending in a nuclear war. Douglas Brode describes the movie in* Films of the Sixties:

[Dr.] *Strangelove's* unexpected success convinced its studio, Columbia, that certain qualities once associated with the underground—anti-Establishment, counterculture, noncommercial filmmakers—were just then reaching the surface, being absorbed by the mainstream. . . . *Strangelove* contained scathing satire of the United States government and military; dark comedy and sick humor; off-color language . . . and a pessimistic ending (the destruction of civilization as we know it) presented . . . [as a] comedy. In short, *Strangelove* contained everything the mass audience would, supposedly, be offended by. . . . Yet, for all that, *Strangelove* was embraced by the American public—a sign that . . . the public was growing more acceptant of ideas and images once thought of as exclusively for [artists and intellectuals]. . . .

[The] viewer is introduced to General Jack D. Ripper . . . , a wild-eyed, old-time right-wing military man, who fervently believes a Communist conspiracy is polluting the body fluids of American citizens. . . . In order to retaliate, he dispatches a fleet of jet bombers—equipped with missiles featuring nuclear warheads—toward Russia, led by the rootin', tootin', shootin' and salutin' Major T. J. "King" Kong . . . , a Texas cowboy turned air force commander who wears his old Stetson on bombing missions. . . .

[Viewers] carried away with them the image of the President's special advisor, Dr. Strangelove . . . , a former Nazi scientist whose mechanical arm constantly slips into an unintentional, uncontrollable "Sieg Heil" salute. . . . With [such] lacerating wit, *Dr. Strangelove* brought sick humor to the commercial cinema.

generation whose adolescent references included one of the great crimes of the century, the assassination of President Kennedy—which, thanks to television, had [practically] taken place before their eyes. . . . [Along] with daily gruesome TV coverage of the Vietnam War, it became impossible to doubt the [vulgar efficiency] of violence. [58]

Breaking Taboos

As the barriers against on-screen violence fell, so too did the taboo against unconventional sexual relationships. The plot of 1967's *The Graduate,* for example, revolved around an all-American college boy who is seduced by an older woman, the wife of his father's wealthy business partner. In 1969, the comedy *Bob & Carol & Ted & Alice* explored taboo issues such as wife-swapping and marijuana smoking. The story is about two middle-class couples who try to embrace the values of the counterculture by purchasing hippie clothing and trying out marijuana and free love. In *Films of the Sixties,* Douglas Brode describes the plot as a "study of early middle-age people who tried to embrace both the new morality and the youth revolution, attempting to reorder their lifestyles to fit in with the breezy image of how liberated people ought to behave." [59]

Another hit film of 1969, the drama *Midnight Cowboy,* was the unflinching story of two down-on-their-luck street hustlers in New York City. One character, Joe Buck, comes to the city from Texas with dreams of becoming a highly paid gigolo to rich New York women. Instead he finds that his cowboy clothes make him much more attractive to gay men. Although tame by today's standards, the film received an "X" rating because it dealt with issues concerning homosexuality. The rating restricted audiences to over age eighteen but did not dampen the critical and popular acclaim or hurt the careers of its two new stars, Dustin Hoffman and Jon Voight.

Born to Be Wild

As movie plots got more daring, so too did the people who wrote, directed, and starred in films. By the late sixties, the reality of life in Hollywood was not far removed from the scenes depicted in *Bob & Carol & Ted & Alice.* And in some cases, it was even less restrained. Many movie stars and filmmakers had tried LSD and lived the hippie lifestyle when they were not on screen.

Two of the most notorious hippies in Hollywood were Dennis Hopper and Peter Fonda, son of film legend Henry Fonda. In 1969, Hopper and Fonda created the film *Easy Rider,* a now-classic icon of sixties culture. The plot revolves around the misadventures of Captain America, played by Fonda, and Billy, played by Hopper, as they journey by motorcycle across the United States. As Fonda describes the story: "The time was right for a really good movie about motorcycles and drugs. . . . These two guys, they score dope, sell everything and split [leave] L.A. for Florida . . . they go across the country, [and] come face to face with themselves." [60] Along the way, the bikers visit a hippie commune in New Mexico, take LSD at the Mardi Gras, and are harassed, beaten, and finally killed by rednecks who despise them for their long hair and counterculture attitudes. Brode analyzes the plot:

Easy Rider is a surprisingly moral tale, for . . . the buying and selling of hard drugs dooms the quest before it starts.

A search for truth cannot be financed by an immoral act without disastrous results. . . . The most important comment *Easy Rider* made was to be found in the vast discrepancy between the visual beauty of the movie . . . and the ugliness of the climate of life in the late Sixties. . . . [For] one brief moment the American cinema was radicalized by the extremity of the times. . . . In 1969, that mood was best exemplified by *Easy Rider*.[61]

Easy Rider had a rock soundtrack that featured some of the biggest artists of the day including Jimi Hendrix, the Band, the Byrds, and Steppenwolf. When it was released, the film, which cost a little more than half a million dollars to make, grossed an incredible $60 million.

Low-Key Antiwar Statements

Much more playful than *Easy Rider, Alice's Restaurant* was probably the first movie based entirely on a popular song. The song, "Alice's Restaurant Massacree," released in 1966, was itself unique. Written by the eighteen-year-old Arlo Guthrie (the son of legendary folksinger Woody Guthrie), the song is over eighteen minutes in length.

Easy Rider *starred Peter Fonda (right) and Dennis Hopper (left) as motorcycle-riding hippies on a cross-country journey. The film was a box-office success, and remains a cult classic.*

In essence, a rambling recitation, Guthrie tells the true story of how he had "a Thanksgiving dinner that couldn't be beat"[62] at a commune run by restauranteur Alice Brock. When dinner was over, Guthrie set out with a Volkswagen vanload of garbage to take to the landfill. Finding it closed for Thanksgiving, Guthrie dumped the garbage by the side of the road. Within hours, the singer is arrested and fined $25 for littering. Later, Guthrie is ordered to appear at a physical for induction into the army. He is deemed morally unfit for service in Vietnam, however, because of his criminal record—for littering.

Guthrie's low-key humor and notable storytelling abilities made "The Alice's Restaurant Massacree" one of the most popular antiwar songs in the United States. It also inspired director Arthur Penn to make a movie of the song immediately after directing *Bonnie and Clyde*. Guthrie stars in the movie with several other non-professional actors. *Alice's Restaurant* featured guitar-toting hippies smoking marijuana and living in a commune housed in an old church. Contrary to popular public opinion of hippies as immoral hedonists, the movie shows its characters to have a high standard of down-to-earth morality. Guthrie believes that war is immoral and is incredulous that a littering conviction makes him unfit to be a soldier. In addition, there is kindness and compassion between the characters as they struggle to help each other through love, death, and other difficulties of life.

James Bond (left, played here by Sean Connery) movies were among the most popular of the 1960s.

A Revolution, American Style

Not all films made in the late 1960s dealt with drugs, hippies, sex, and antiwar themes. In fact, some of the most popular movies featured James Bond playing British secret agent 007. These films, such as *Goldfinger* and *Dr. No*, found the unflappable Bond, played by Sean Connery, facing off against evil madmen bent on destroying the world. Many of these villains and their henchmen resembled leaders of Communist countries such as the Soviet Union and China thus reflecting the Cold War mentality that characterized American politics in the 1960s.

Traditional American values were also seen in the movies starring tough guy John "Duke" Wayne, who was a strong supporter of the war in Vietnam. Wayne starred in and codirected the movie *Green Berets* in 1968, in which, according to Edelstein, the "Duke as a Green Beret colonel defends the American way and convinces a typically smarmy U.S. journalist . . . of the rightness of our presence in Vietnam."[63]

Such movies were in the minority, however, in the era remembered for drugs, sex, and rock and roll. And although Hollywood made little notice of the drastic changes sweeping across the globe until the last part of the decade, filmmakers made up for lost time between 1967 and 1969. As Biskind writes:

Because movies are expensive and time-consuming to make, Hollywood is always the last to know, the slowest to respond, and in those years it was at least half a decade behind the other popular arts. So it was some time before the acrid odor of cannabis [marijuana] and tear gas wafted over the pools of Beverly Hills and the sounds of shouting reached the studio gates. But when flower power finally hit in the late '60s, it hit hard. As America burned, Hells Angels gunned their bikes down Sunset Boulevard, while girls danced topless in the street to the music of the Doors booming from the clubs that lined [Sunset] Strip. . . . It was one long party. Everything old was bad, everything new was good. Nothing was sacred; everything was up for grabs. It was, in fact, a cultural revolution, American style.[64]

Chapter 5

Television Comes of Age

By the 1960s, television was the main source of entertainment and information for most Americans. The growing influence of TV can be tracked by looking at the number of sets in American homes. In 1946—when the first baby boomers were born—only 7,000 TV sets existed in the United States. By 1950, 4.4 million families were tuning in to the wonders of television. In 1960, Americans owned 50 million televisions and 90 percent of American homes had at least one TV. By the mid-sixties, small "portable" televisions had been introduced, allowing each family member to have his or her own TV. At that time, the average American watched television at least six hours a day.

Although it was a relatively new form of entertainment, the power of TV cannot be underestimated. When sociologist Gary Steiner interviewed twenty-five hundred Americans in 1960, he found that by a large majority, the average "viewer finds television an important and positive contribution to everyday life—in fact, [viewers] name it as the single development of the past 25 years that has done the most to make life more enjoyable, pleasant, and interesting. . . . As compared with radio, magazines and newspapers, television is far and away the [most enjoyed] entertainment medium. And this is true all the way across the educational ladder. All viewers—highbrows [intellectuals] included—agree that television is the most entertaining." [65]

Pleasing the Audience

As Steiner shows, the influence of television cut across all levels of society. For the entire decade, however, before the introduction of cable TV, there were only three television networks and thus only three television channels in most cities. Some rural areas only had one or two television channels, and in extremely isolated places no television was available at all. Since VCRs, DVDs, and home computers did not yet exist, almost everything Americans watched at home was broadcast by the big three networks: NBC, CBS, and ABC. These networks had their own news divisions, and programming ranged from variety shows and children's cartoons and comedies to westerns, police dramas, and sports.

Then as now, the networks were in business to make money through the sale of advertising time, broadcasting commercials during and between programs. As ABC vice president Donald Coyle stated in the early sixties, television was meant to "fulfill its natural function as a giant pump fueling the machine of consumer demand, stepping up the flow of goods and services to keep living standards high and the economy expanding." [66]

With such an attitude, it is not surprising that television programs were aimed at pleasing the largest possible mass audience. Particular care was taken not to offend anyone, especially those middle- and upper-class audiences cherished by the advertisers.

More than any other medium, television enforced the values of the majority of Americans. In the early sixties, this led to shows that featured tough-talking cowboys engaged in gunfights with villains in black hats. Between 1960 and 1962, the four most popular shows on TV were the westerns *Gunsmoke; Wagon Train; Have Gun, Will Travel;* and *Bonanza.*

Bonanza, a series about a father and three sons in the Cartwright family, was the most-watched TV show between 1964 and 1967. In *60s!* John and Gordon Javna explain how this show symbolized America's shared values:

By the 1960s, television had become the primary form of entertainment in America.

Actors Andy Griffith (left), Don Knotts (center), and Ron Howard (right) starred in the popular situation-comedy series The Andy Griffith Show.

[The Cartwrights] played fair and they worked hard. They were humble, they went to church, and yet, they had a sense of humor. . . . They were kind to strangers. They stood up for the underdog, they cared about people. And they were . . . rich. . . . "Bonanza" was so popular that people often refused to believe that [their ranch called] the Ponderosa was fictional.[67]

By the mid-1960s, however, cowboy shows gave way to situation comedies, many of which, notably *The Andy Griffith Show*, poked gentle fun at small-town America and the American dream. One of the most popular shows of the 1960s was *The Beverly Hillbillies*, about a family of poor backwoods "mountaineers," the Clampetts, who become fabulously rich when they strike oil on their farm, then move to America's richest neighborhood, Beverly Hills, in Los Angeles, California. Plots generally pitted naiveté and ignorance against city slickers, and as often as not, country ways outwitted the rich folks. Although critics panned

The Beverly Hillbillies *was a popular series about the misadventures of the backwoods Clampett family in Beverly Hills.*

the show, average Americans loved it, keeping it in the top twenty most-popular shows from 1962 to 1969.

During this era, California had become the most populous state in the country, and millions of people were moving there every year. And, as David Farber writes in *The Great Age of Dreams: America in the 1960s:*

> Like the Clampetts, people from diverse backgrounds had uprooted themselves, left their kinfolk and community behind them, and started life anew in California.
> . . .
>
> Just as important, the Clampetts' sudden wealth served as a fun-house mirror for the relatively new prosperity millions of Americans enjoyed by the

early 1960s. While few viewers could expect a Beverly Hills mansion, many who had lived through the Great Depression in urban tenements or broken-down farmhouses did find themselves living in all-electric California-style ranch houses and were aware of the distance they had traveled. [68]

Sixties television sometimes had a dark side, however, that revealed some of the negative aspects of American society. *The Twilight Zone,* which aired on Friday nights from 1959 to 1962, used science-fiction-based stories to expose the follies of racism, mob violence, materialism, and the dangers of rigid conformity. Although the show, with its robots, devils, and creatures from other planets, had a cult following, it did not last long in the optimistic sixties. Most Americans preferred tough cowboys and bumbling hillbillies to the weightier lessons of *The Twilight Zone.*

Cartoons on TV

In the 1950s, animated cartoons were mainly geared toward young children. As the baby boomers reached their teen years, however, cartoons came to be seen as entertainment for both old and young. Modeled on sitcoms such as *The Beverly Hillbillies,* sixties cartoon families were also seen as reflecting middle-class American values.

From 1960 to 1966, *The Flintstones* was an enormously popular cartoon show, and the first to run in prime time—the hours between 7 and 10 P.M. In *Sixties People,* Jane and Michael Stern write that the show was so well loved because Americans saw themselves reflected in this "modern Stone Age family."

"The Flintstones" was . . . about [an average] suburban family . . . except for the twist that they live in the Stone Age. [The characters] ride in stone cars, speak on stone telephones, play "rock" music on a turntable that uses a prehistoric bird's beak for a needle, and . . . have all the modern [features] of suburbia, including bowling night, home swimming pools, baby sitting, dogs, etc. [Father] Fred is a construction worker; the motto of the company where he works is "Own Your Own Cave and Be Secure."[69]

With the success of *The Flintstones,* producers of the show launched another cartoon in 1962. *The Jetsons* were also an average middle-class family but lived in the distant future. Stone and wood were

TV and the Space Age

Some of the most memorable televised events of the sixties combined news and entertainment as Americans followed the progress of the Mercury, Gemini, and Apollo space missions. In a 1961 speech before Congress, President John F. Kennedy promised that the United States would put a man on the moon by 1970. Although the Soviet Union had sent the first man into space in 1961, it became imperative to Americans that the United States be the first to reach the moon. For the rest of the decade, a majority of Americans paid close attention to the "space race" against the Soviet Union. And the place where they were able to follow the progress was on their TV sets.

For most Americans, the space age began on television in 1961 when millions of people watched the televised blastoff of a spacecraft holding Alan Shepard. He traveled in a space capsule a mere 300 miles in suborbital flight, becoming the first U.S. astronaut in space. On February 20, 1962, when John Glenn orbited the earth at a speed of 17,500 miles per hour, the entire country came to a standstill as millions of Americans gathered around their TVs to follow Glenn's progress. Church bells rang joyously across the country upon his successful landing. After the mission, Glenn was treated as an American hero. He received a ticker-tape parade in New York City, another televised event.

On July 21, 1969, the technological wonder of television was magnified once again as Neil Armstrong became the first man to walk on the moon. Tens of millions of people all over the world watched Armstrong take those first tentative steps on live TV.

transformed to ultramodern metal and plastic as the Jetsons traveled in rocket-ship cars, were waited on by a robot maid, and had meals prepared in a fully automatic robotic kitchen. Like the Flintstones, the Jetsons were just like the viewers, only living in different eras. As the Sterns write: "Thus, [they] could bask in the monotony of their own lives playing out in centuries past and future, the implication being that civilization as they knew it, in all its comfortable mediocrity, would never end."[70]

Aliens and Witches

Humorous science-fiction themes in a middle-class setting were also played out in nonanimated shows. For example, *My Favorite Martian* follows the story of an average man and his roommate, a Martian, who looks human but possesses superpowers.

Another popular sixties show was *Bewitched*, which first aired in 1964. This sitcom combined a science-fiction theme, middle-class values, and a growing sense that a woman could be in charge of her own life without help from her husband. The show followed the life of a typical housewife, with a twist: Samantha Stephens was a powerful witch married to a stereotypical, middle-class man, Darren. Samantha created constant comical mischief with her superpowers much to the chagrin of Darren. This portrayal of an all-powerful woman in control of her family's destiny had feminist overtones during a time when the idea of women's liberation was taking hold in America. Adam Blair explains on the Harpies Bizarre website:

"Bewitched" is clearly a parable for feminism. A strong, confident, capable woman with enormous powers is literally roped into domestication. Her husband, under the guise of protecting their marriage and maintaining his own status, forbids her from using those powers. How many women still feel straight-jacketed by their mates' narrow view of their proper roles? . . . "Bewitched" premiered in 1964, and women's liberation blossomed into a potent force during its run—with nary an on-screen mention. It wasn't nec-

The science-fiction themed series Bewitched *carried strong feminist overtones.*

essary, and indeed would have made the tensions on the show unbearable: the battle was being played out already, week after week.[71]

Sharing Common Experiences

Sociologists have speculated that *Bewitched* was popular (and is so today) because many viewers wish they could use powers like Samantha's to control their lives. For this reason, the show served as a minor distraction in a turbulent decade. But television also played an important role in bringing people together and letting them share common experiences in times of tragedy. This sense of immediacy and collective experience was never more keen than on November 22, 1963, when President John F. Kennedy was assassinated in Dallas, Texas. In what was perhaps the main television event of the 1960s, more than 175 million people—93 percent of all Americans— watched the events that followed on television. All three major networks suspended regular programming—and all commercials— to broadcast the breaking news. Two days later, Lee Harvey Oswald, Kennedy's alleged assassin, was himself shot on live television as police were transferring Oswald from the Dallas County Jail.

Almost everyone in America saw Oswald being shot as it happened—a first in television history. Because of the power of television, these two bizarre murders seemed to collectively shatter America's postwar innocence. As sixties antiwar leader Tom Hayden later wrote: "We followed the breaking news,

Millions of Americans watched President John F. Kennedy's funeral procession on television in November 1963.

watched the murder of Oswald over and over [on television], and let the event etch its way like a toxic acid into our consciousness. This was the most unexpected happening of my life, having been raised in the climate of a stable American presidency . . . in an unstable and warring world."[72]

On Sunday, November 24, with the Thanksgiving holiday only days away, almost everyone in America watched Kennedy's funeral on television. After America's youngest president was laid to rest, regular TV programming resumed. A following study by Social Research Inc. stated that the decision to return to regular broadcasting after more than two hundred hours of commercial-free coverage of Kennedy's death, "set an orderly limit on the period of mourning and told the public, now we should all get back to the task of living."[73]

The televised violence surrounding Kennedy's death was unprecedented but soon occurred with sickening regularity as the Vietnam War became the most gripping "show" on television. A new generation of smaller cameras allowed reporters to broadcast immediate and unparalleled coverage of the war. For the first time in history, civilians far from the battlefields could view burning villages, anguished peasants, bloody American soldiers, and other graphic horrors of war. Whether this coverage turned public opinion against the war remains an unanswered and hotly debated question. During the second part of the decade, however, watching the televised war on dinner-hour news programs was a daily event for millions of Americans. For those who opposed the war, it reinforced their sense of commitment to bring it to an end.

Voices of the Counterculture

Antiwar sentiments combined with the widespread use of LSD put the counterculture at the forefront of societal change. By 1969, hippies were seen everywhere, there were riots in urban neighborhoods and demonstrations on college campuses, and typical middle-class Americans saw a world transformed almost beyond recognition.

While news programs sometimes showed hippies frolicking in a park—or protesting in front of the White House—the bulk of prime-time television remained as noncontroversial as ever. Social commentary was confined to books and magazines, underground newspapers, music, alternative theater, and an occasional Hollywood movie.

In February 1967, prime-time TV was jolted out of its conformity when *The Smothers Brothers Comedy Hour* premiered on CBS. Airing during the most violent years of an already tumultuous decade, *The Smothers Brothers Comedy Hour* provided a network voice for the antiwar, antiestablishment elements of society. This was at a time when a majority of Americans still supported U.S. involvement in the Vietnam War.

The hosts of the show, Tom and Dick Smothers, were as unlikely a pair of agitators as had ever appeared on-screen. With conservative suits and short hair, the straight-laced duo had previously gained fame as joke-telling folksingers. The brothers were hired by CBS to knock NBC's *Bonanza* out of the number-one slot, an unenviable task that had proved impossible for others. CBS believed that the conservative appearance of the Smothers brothers would appeal to middle-class America, while their offbeat humor might attract young people who, at the time, were turning away from TV in droves. To pull in both audiences, the *Smothers Brothers* booked a mix of older Hollywood stars such as Bette Davis, George Burns, and Jack Benny with new talent such as George Carlin, Simon and Garfunkel, and Sonny and Cher. The formula worked, and the *Smothers Brothers* quickly knocked *Bonanza* out of first place. CBS, however, got more than it bargained for.

"Hippies with Haircuts"

Tom and Dick Smothers described themselves as "hippies with haircuts,"[74] and they quickly upset CBS censors and conservative Americans in several ways.

One controversial recurring skit featured comedian Leigh French, who played a character named Goldie O'Keefe. Goldie was a stereotypical "hippie chick" with wide eyes, long braids, and beads. She was also obviously acting as if she were high on marijuana. Her parody of an afternoon talk show for housewives, "Share a Little Tea with Goldie," opened with the pun "Hi[gh]! And glad of it!"[75] The skit took advantage of the fact that few Americans were aware of this drug slang at the time, as Aniko Bodroghkozy writes:

Terms such as "roach," "head," "tea," (and, for that matter, "Goldie" . . .) all had drug-oriented meanings within countercultural circles. The show's facility with the current slang may have assisted in legitimizing its material with young people and mystifying its meanings to the older generation. [CBS] may have realized that many of these terms were drug code words, but seemed incapable of preventing all the

The Smothers brothers described themselves as "hippies with haircuts." During the late 1960s their show, The Smothers Brothers Comedy Hour, *was the voice of American counterculture.*

"roaches" from sneaking through. The slang and punning use of language became a means to evade the network's policing. Young "heads" could take pleasure from the broadcasting of celebratory references to drugs, supposedly taboo on network television. [76]

While sly pot humor was allowed to slip by the censors, the Smothers brothers also created controversy with their choice of musical guests. When the San Francisco band the Jefferson Airplane appeared on the show, singer Grace Slick painted her face black and raised her fist in a "black power" salute as she sang.

Commercializing the Counterculture

Sixties television producers shied away from controversial subjects so as not to offend corporations that paid for commercials. Ironically, those very commercials contained an increasing dose of sexual titillation, drug references, and rock music. Patrick Walsh explored this phenomenon in a 1969 TV Guide *article reprinted in Barry G. Cole's* Television:

[Television] is changing faster than at any other period in its history. . . . It is in the commercials that the revolutions . . . can be most easily observed. I refer, of course, to the drug prevalence, the sexual revolution, and the massive alterations in the way people look, dress and act—the new freedom. . . .

In a nation taught to have a horror of drugs . . . which has traditionally had a phobia about sex . . . and which has emphasized conformity in both dress and hair, commercials are mirroring some strange things indeed.

According to a Bufferin [aspirin] commercial, "It's a turned-on day". . . . Pepsi comes to the rescue because it, according to the commercials, "turns you on". . . . If your kid drops acid or blows a little pot to get turned on, it is obviously not a Good Thing. But what about that turned-on world we accept [in commercial products]?

And why should a guy get expelled from school, threatened and cajoled by his parents and bugged by half of society because he has long hair, when whole gangs of people are on television peddling [products] to hold down your [Beatlesque hair]. . . .

[Today's commercials] display an . . . open sexuality which are incongruous in relation to most other television programming, and, indeed, to much of American society.

In 1968, the Smothers brothers booked folksinger Pete Seeger who, because of his leftist political views, had been blacklisted—that is, kept off of TV—since the 1950s. After a long fight with censors, Seeger was allowed to sing his antiwar song "Waist Deep in the Big Muddy"—about a gung-ho military officer during World War II who forces his men to cross a raging river only to be drowned in the muddy waters. This was seen by many as a commentary on President Johnson's policies in Vietnam. Another antiwar activist, Joan Baez, was censored when she tried to dedicate a song to her husband, David Harris, who was in prison at the time for refusing orders to be drafted into the army.

By this time, the confrontation seen in the streets between protesters and police was mirrored at CBS as the stars and writers of the *Smothers Brothers* vehemently fought television executives and censors. Meanwhile, the show was receiving mailbags full of angry letters from outraged viewers across the nation. Even the newly elected president, Richard Nixon, jumped into the fray in early 1969. Nixon called top CBS executives and pressured them to cancel the show. The president made a case to CBS that he did not want a weekly comedy series making fun of his administration and questioning his aggressive policies in Vietnam.

For this and other reasons, CBS responded by canceling the show. It was replaced by *Hee Haw,* a variety show that featured country-music stars, country comedians, and scantily clad women in short shorts and straw hats making corny jokes. The skits often took place on sets such as front porches, corn fields, log cabins, and barns that were a call to America's nostalgic rural past. Protest marches, Vietnam, and Nixon's policies were never mentioned on *Hee Haw,* and the brief heyday of counterculture TV provided by the *Smothers Brothers* was over.

Laughing with *Laugh-In*

While the *Smothers Brothers* used comedy for political ends, a 1968 show, *Rowan & Martin's Laugh-In,* used politics as a springboard to comedy. While *Laugh-In* slyly celebrated the counterculture and made fun of political issues, it was much more lighthearted than *The Smothers Brothers Comedy Hour.*

Laugh-In was hosted by a pair of former lounge comedians, Dan Rowan and Dick Martin, and derived its title from the Human Be-In, a counterculture celebration held in San Francisco in January 1967. The show featured a flood of one-liner jokes, running skits, and musical numbers. Unique for the time, editors spliced as many as five hundred different scenes together to give the show a fast-paced feel commonly seen today in music videos and elsewhere. Dick Martin explains how the show broke many other traditional boundaries:

> Yes, we broke a lot of barriers. For instance, people didn't realize you couldn't do pregnancy jokes when we did them. [Comedian] Joanne Worley standing, obviously pregnant, at the crook of the piano singing, "I should

have danced all night." We did a lot of them. We broke the marijuana ban. In one show, Judy Carne said, "my boyfriend's so dumb he thinks a little pot is Tupperware for midgets." Then we had one of those streamers going across the screen that said, "For the first time in the history of the United States, everyone has agreed on everything and they walked out with their arms around each other. The officials are still looking to find out who put the grass in the air-conditioner." The censor didn't know what it meant. He came and asked "What's so funny about putting grass in the air-conditioner." We said, "Trust us, it's funny." [77]

Laugh-In was also the first to create catchphrases that were repeated every week. Before long, these phrases such as "verrrrrr-y interesting," "ring my chimes," "sock it to me," "you bet your sweet bippy," and "here come the judge!" became part of the American lexicon. They were seen on lunch boxes, bumper stickers, buttons, and T-shirts.

Black and White on TV

While Laugh-In changed the way television programs could look and sound, another revolution was taking place on the airwaves in the 1960s. By 1969, African Americans were starring in two dozen prime-time shows including spy dramas such as I Spy and Mission: Impossible, comedies such as Julia, and variety shows like the Sammy Davis, Jr. Show, the Leslie Uggams Show, and the Flip Wilson Show. African Americans also costarred in shows such as Hogan's Heroes, Star Trek, Rowan and Martin's Laugh-In, Mannix, and Peyton Place. This was in stark contrast to 1965 when studies showed only three black people appeared on-screen during an average evening, and of those, two were on for less than one minute. And the new shows, according J. Fred MacDonald in Blacks and White TV, were "practically free of stereotyping," [78] unlike earlier years when black people were usually relegated to playing butlers, maids, or criminals.

These changes have led some to call the late sixties the "Golden Age of Blacks in Television." [79] In Television, Barry G. Cole explains why this phenomenon occurred:

The reasons commonly given for the large increase in the appearance of blacks on television in 1968–69 were several. These included the pressure of social change which was accelerated by the civil rights movement; the success of Bill Cosby in I Spy, [an official government report] which charged TV with "tending to ignore the fact that an appreciable part of its audience is black" and called for the use of more black actors; the assassination of Martin Luther King; an increasing recognition by advertisers of the buying power of blacks and the ability of television to reach them; and finally, as one reporter put it, "a willingness on the industry's part to further the cause of social justice as long as it is in vogue and doesn't cost money." [80]

As Cole mentions, *I Spy* was one of the reasons attitudes changed about African Americans on TV. The show, a spy thriller starring Bill Cosby as a secret agent, was the first prime-time drama to star a black actor. Before coming to the show, Cosby mined his childhood and family for humor. His dramatic acting in *I Spy*, however, was very well received, and he won an Emmy Award for best actor in every one of the three years the show ran. MacDonald offers praise for Cosby's role:

> Cosby's character [Alexander Scott] was always equal to his encounters with foreign agents, heads of state, beautiful women, and would-be murderers. He was unlike Shaft, Superfly, and other exaggerated "superspade" characters developed in the so-called blaxploitation films of the next decade. Alexander Scott was a real, mature human character—able to feel and express emotions historically forbidden to black characters in mainstream entertainment media.[81]

I Spy broke a long-standing taboo against showing on-screen interracial romance. In one episode, Cosby's character falls in love with a white female secret agent and the two were shown kissing, touching, and caressing each other. Not everyone accepted such scenes, however. Station owners in three southern cities, Savannah and Albany, Georgia, and Daytona Beach, Florida, refused to run *I Spy*. NBC, however, had actually antici-

Starring Bill Cosby and Robert Culp, I Spy *was one of the first television series to feature a black actor in a leading role.*

pated a larger negative reaction, and for three years the show was seen in 96 percent of the country on 180 other stations.

Middle-Class Controversy

While *I Spy* was widely accepted, another show with a black star, *Julia,* faced problems. And it was African Americans who complained about this show. *Julia* starred Diahann Carroll as Julie Baker, a beautiful, middle-class widow working as a nurse and raising a young son. Plot lines were very similar to other situation comedies at the time. But because *Julia* made no references to racial issues, she was called a "white Negro"[82] by her critics. This was in 1968, the year Martin Luther King Jr. was assassinated, urban neighborhoods were inflamed by riots, and many African Americans were embracing "black power" and the militant agenda

of the Black Panthers. MacDonald explains why this was a problem for the show:

There is an aspect to most black performance in popular culture which is unique. Because there [was] comparatively little minority representation in . . . television, and because each performance by an Afro-American is

Women on Television

In 1964, feminist author Betty Friedan wrote a scathing commentary for TV Guide *on the stereotypical roles of women seen in television commercials. It was reprinted in* Television, *edited by Barry G. Cole.*

If the image of women on television today reflects—or affects—reality, then American women must be writhing in agonies of self-contempt and unappeasable sexual hunger. For television's image of the American woman is a stupid, unattractive, insecure little household drudge who spends her martyred, mindless, boring days dreaming of love—and plotting nasty revenge against her husband. . . .

This is the rather horrifying feeling I had after sitting for several weeks in front of my television set, trying to reconcile the image of woman projected by television commercials and family situation comedies, by soap operas and game shows . . . with the . . . virtually nonexistent image of woman in all the rest of television: the major dramatic shows, the witty commentary, serious documentary or ordinary reportage of the issues and news of our world. . . .

Consider first that drab, repulsive little housewife one sees on the television screen. She is so stupid that she is barely capable of doing the most menial household tasks. Her biggest problem is to get the kitchen sink or floor really clean, and she can't even do that without a kind, wise man to tell her how. . . .

Less than a fifth grader, more like a simple animal . . . this television-commercial woman has no interest, purpose or goal beyond cleaning her sink, feeding her kids, and going to bed. The whole world beyond her home—its politics, art, science, issues, ideas and problems—is evidently beyond her comprehension.

regarded as a chance to make a statement about black realities, each appearance takes on added weight. . . . If a role seems too accepting of white social dominance, the star as well as the character he or she is portraying may be attacked as too [compliant]. If the role is one of a middleclass suburban black, it may be assailed as too [conventional] and unsympathetic to inner-city "brothers" and "sisters." If the role involves no racial politics, it may be censured as not "black" enough. And if it is critical of social injustice, it may be assailed [by white viewers] as hostile, radical, or heavy-handed.

In effect, in the late 1960s, whenever a black entertainer appeared, he or she was expected to represent all Afro-Americans, embodying the panorama of black life from slum to suburb. Because of its patent failure to do this, no successful black series was more controversial than *Julia*.[83]

These controversies bothered Carroll, and she refused to continue the show in 1971 although it was popular, pulling in a respectable 14 million viewers every week.

"Vast Wasteland"

As in any era, television in the sixties was mostly harmless drivel, what Newton Minow, chairman of the Federal Communications Commission, called a "vast wasteland"[84] in 1961. In the last third of the decade, however, people became increasingly sensitive to various social and political problems in America. On occasion, these sympathies were expressed on television. More often than not, however, TV remained as noncontroversial as possible. With hillbillies, Martians, and Stone Age families, TV was a constant source of traditional values as the world outside the box changed dramatically.

Toys, Fads, and Fashion

Every era has its fads and fashions; in the 1960s, consumer trends were determined by the young. With 75 million baby boomers between kindergarten and college age, this huge population "bubble" influenced everything from the sale of Superballs to the length of womens' skirts. And, like the Superball, the fads and fashions of the 1960s keep bouncing back to influence the way Americans look and play. For example, "hip-hugger" jeans are probably more popular today then they were during the "summer of love" in 1967. Tie-dyed T-shirts that were said to represent the colors of an acid trip are now sold in shopping malls and discount stores. Some men continue to wear their hair long, while beards have become acceptable on everyone from businessmen to TV newscasters. Fads of the sixties, such as skateboards and surfing, have become an ingrained part of America's youth culture.

Barbie's Dreams of the Future

With nearly 4 million children born every year in the United States throughout the fifties, the toy business was expanding at an extraordinary rate. But Ruth Handler, founder of Mattel Toys, believed that some children's needs were not being met.

In 1959, Handler noticed that her daughter, Barbara, was playing with paper dolls and trying to dress them in cutout paper clothes. The toy maker realized that little girls like playing "dress up." The popular dolls of the time, however, were babies that did not have wardrobes. Handler decided to create a three-dimensional doll that her daughter could relate to as she grew older, not a baby doll, but something that would "project every little girl's dream of the future."[85] Handler came up with Barbie, the first mass-produced doll with an adult woman's body.

At first, critics said the adult-proportioned Barbie was immodest and inappropriate for young girls. This did not stop little girls from demanding that their parents buy the doll, however, and Barbie was an instant hit. To increase profits, Handler had dozens of outfits designed for the doll. This allowed young girls to participate in fashion trends, dressing their Barbies in outfits that they themselves hoped to buy as they grew older. Aimed squarely at middle-class, suburban girls, Barbie could be dressed for a slumber party, tennis match, football outing, ballet recital, nightclub performance, or her own wedding. And Mattel paid close attention to detail. Barbie's outfits had working zippers and buttons, hand-sewn labels, and other details of fine fashion.

While the Barbie doll was sold for only $3, each piece of clothing could cost from $1 to $5. Barbie's entire wardrobe could be obtained for $136, this at a time when the

Despite their high cost and criticism that the dolls were inappropriate for young girls, Barbie dolls were very popular throughout the 1960s.

average middle-class worker earned less than $100 a week. Despite the high cost to the consumer, in 1965 Mattel sold more than $100 million worth of Barbie merchandise and became the biggest toy maker in the world.

By that time Barbie had a house, a car, and a boyfriend named Ken. But the real world was changing rapidly, and Mattel struggled to update Barbie but still retain her wholesome image. Kristin Riddick explains how this was done on the Inventing Barbie website:

[Barbie] needed to show America that although the country was in political turmoil, she presented a stable yet still incredibly fashionable lifestyle. . . . The pearls were abandoned for bright, dangling earrings, and Barbie donned a mini skirt with her newly-designed bent legs! But she could not do it alone. Francie, Barbie's "modern cousin," was introduced in a polka-dotted top and gingham bikini bottom in 1966 . . . and Ken was back, after a brief absence, with a new face and a more "mod" haircut. The friends allowed Barbie to wear more faddish clothes; she was jazzy, cool, even "zingy."

Although the new outfits suggested excitement and adventure, the series and titles were named for the fabrics instead of the activities. Outfits like "Fur Out" and "Mini Print" assured the public that Barbie was not . . . wandering around in a drug-induced daze. . . . Through Barbie, Mattel portrayed

not only what society's expectations were . . . but they now showed the alternatives to the controversial activities that appeared to be in the limelight. Society expects her to be participating in the same kind of activities that the majority of the teenagers were doing: smoking marijuana, practicing "free love," and protesting on the White House Lawn. Mattel presented her as the ideal modern teenager; she normalized mini skirts and go go boots because they did not accompany drugs and protests in her representation of the era. Parents found a certain sanctuary in Barbie, and they could feel confident that their daughters would not be corrupted by Barbie's activities. [86]

By changing her outfits to fit the times, Barbie's popularity never waned. Since she was invented in 1959, more than 100 million Barbie dolls have been sold throughout the world.

Action Toys

While little girls played with their Barbie dolls, toys made for boys seemed to be getting faster—and even a little bit dangerous. The SuperBall, for example, bounced higher and faster than any other, but could leave nasty welts on those who failed to get out of the way of the space-age ball.

The SuperBall was the accidental invention of Norman Stingley, a California chemist who worked for the Bettis Rubber Company. In his spare time, Stingley created a substance he called Zectron by compressing synthetic

Troll Dolls

In the 1960s, millions of young girls purchased the glamorous Barbie doll. For a few years, however, Barbie's main competition was the troll, a fat, ugly, little doll with a shock of Day-Glo hair. Mark Long describes the popular troll doll on the Bad Fads website:

The Troll Doll was originally known as the "Dammit" doll in honor of its creator, Danish wood-cutter Thomas Dam. In 1959, Dam could not afford to buy his young daughter a birthday present and instead carved for her a doll inspired by the legendary trolls which were believed to live in the Nordic forests and would bring luck to any humans who could catch them. Dam's daughter took to the doll and dressed it up and showed it to local villagers. The doll attracted the eye of a Danish toy store owner and soon Dam was selling versions of the doll all over the world, selling more than a million of them in the United States in 1964 alone.

Part of the dolls charm was that it was so ugly—it had huge ears and a pot belly, no forehead and long strands of sheep's wool for hair. Danes believed the dolls were so ugly that you had to laugh at them and if you were laughing, nothing bad could happen to you. Soon the dolls became a source of good luck to people around the world. Initially they were favored by high school and college girls but soon grown men were carrying them around on their travels.

rubber under thirty-five hundred pounds of pressure per square inch. Because Zectron tended to chip easily, however, the inventor could find no industrial application for it.

Stingley took Zectron to Wham-O Manufacturing, the company that had made millions of dollars in the late fifties marketing hula hoops and Frisbees. Within months, Wham-O turned Zectron into the SuperBall, a 98-cent, plum-sized ball with an amazing ability to bounce. A SuperBall dropped from shoulder height would jump back to 92 percent of the original distance from which it was dropped—three times more bounce than a tennis ball. In addition, a SuperBall could bounce for a full minute after it was dropped. With such amazing properties, the SuperBall was an instant hit among consumers as Richard A. Johnson explains in *American Fads:*

Uses were many and varied. Super-Balls were bounced over rooftops, dribbled by skateboarders, [and] ricocheted among adjoining surfaces. . . . The tightly compacted, high friction ball could also be spun into a wall in such a way that it would bounce back at the barrier repeatedly. Accomplished SuperBall players could make the self-perpetuating rubber missile hammer itself into a wall four or five times. Long lobbing covered entire city blocks, as the balls ate up the distance with kangaroo-like bounds and seemed to gather momentum as they skipped along the street. Kids also took up baseball bats and entertained [baseball] fantasies by hitting suborbital shots.

Juvenile games were inventive, but adults thought up ways of using Super Balls too. At the workplace they were vaulted over rows of office desktops, sent hopping down corridors, and dropped onto sidewalks and parking lots from windows several stories high. Competitors tried depositing them into far-off wastebaskets with one strategic bounce. [87]

SuperBalls were not just for average office workers. Presidential aide McGeorge Bundy bought sixty SuperBalls for White House staffers. Workers on the Pacific Stock Exchange played with SuperBalls between stock trades.

Nineteen sixty-five was the year of the SuperBall, and more than 7 million were sold by Christmas of that year. At the height of the fad, Wham-O was producing SuperBalls in five separate factories, making up to 170,000 a day. By the end of 1966, however, the SuperBall fad was over. But, as Johnson writes, "no one who ever owned a Super Ball has forgotten the greatest bouncer of all time. No

ball in history ever behaved like the Super Ball and none ever sold like it." [88]

Slot Cars

The same year that SuperBalls bounced into American backyards, millions of dollars were being spent on slot car racing. At a time when many baby boomers were eagerly awaiting their first driver's licenses, these slot cars provided an outlet for speeding, cornering, and other driving skills.

Slot cars are miniature copies of race cars produced in 1/87 to 1/24 scale. Each car has a small fin under the front that fits into a slot on a tabletop race course. Copper strips run parallel to the slot and make contact with an electric motor that propels the slot car. The driver determines the speed of the car with a handheld control that plugs into the track. If the slot car were as large as a real automobile, it would be traveling at the equivalent of six hundred miles per hour. The twists and turns in the track force the driver to carefully control the car or it will fly out of the slot and spin out of control.

In 1965 alone, more than three hundred slot car tracks opened in California, with thousands more taking over storefronts across the United States. Cars modeled on Corvettes, Maseratis, and Mustangs cost anywhere from $3 to $8, and about 3.5 million mostly teenage boys raced them regularly. Five thousand clubs dedicated to slot car racing formed throughout the country. Makers of tracks, cars, and accessories sold $150 million worth of products, more money than Americans spent on golf, skiing, and surfing that year.

The best slot car tracks cost more than $8,000, were over two hundred feet long, with up to eight lanes, several levels, and figure-eight configurations. The edges were decorated like miniature raceways with pit stops and tiny bleachers filled with little people. Anyone with a $1.50 could race for an hour, and an extra 50 cents rented a car. Those who wanted to practice at home could buy a two-lane track for around $20.

Not all slot car racers were kids, however. Celebrities such as newscaster Walter Cronkite, singer Mel Tormé, and Attorney General Robert Kennedy professed their love for slot car racing. In addition, race teams formed at universities such as Princeton, UCLA, Yale, Harvard, and elsewhere. Engineering students and teachers devised ways to soup up their slots by building lightweight chassis, treating tires for traction, and rewinding the coils in the tiny electric motors. These cars were often entered in competitions; in San Francisco alone, nine tournaments were held every weekend during the summer of 1965. The biggest races paid out prizes that ranged from twenty-eight thousand to one hundred thousand dollars.

Crowds of young men race slot cars at a San Francisco tournament. The biggest slot car tournaments offered considerable prize money to the victor.

Surfing, Skateboards, and the Beach Boys

Slot cars were popular for several years, but by 1970, the fad was over and most slot car tracks went out of business. But surfing, another fad that gripped America in the sixties, was still going strong.

Natives of the Hawaiian Islands have been surfing for thousands of years. The idea did not become a fad, however, until the 1960s. At that time, surfing was propelled into the public consciousness by a slew of surfer movies such as *Beach Blanket Bingo*.

(Before 1960, there were a total of ten movies about surfing; by 1969, there were seventy-two.) Surf music, a craze in itself, also helped sell the fad. Bands like Dick Dale and the Del-Tones, the Beach Boys, Jan and Dean, and the Rivieras scored national number-one radio hits with songs such as "Pipeline," "Surfin' Safari," "Surfer's Stomp," "Surfin' USA," "Wipe Out," "Surfin' Bird," and "California Sun."

The surfing fad boomed between 1960 and 1965, at a time when millions were abandoning the dirty, crowded cities of the

The Mustang Gallops Across America

By 1964, millions of baby boomers were getting ready to buy their first cars before going away to college. That same year, Ford unveiled the Mustang. With its bucket seats, racing wheels, and running-pony logo on the console, the car became an instant classic among college-bound teens. The Mustang was fast and sporty yet inexpensive. The economically minded could buy the car with a smaller 6-cylinder engine, while those with extra money could get a powerful V-8 convertible.

Like other sixties fads, people went a little bit crazy over the Mustang. In 1964, when it was used as a pace car at a racetrack in Alabama, thousands of people jumped over a wall and onto the track to gawk at the car. When the first Mustang appeared at a Chicago Ford dealer, the owner was forced to lock the doors of the showroom because so many people were pushing and shoving to get in. In New Jersey, as fifteen buyers fought over a single Mustang, the dealer decided to auction the car off to the highest bidder. The winner then slept in the car until his check cleared.

The Mustang fad quickly set records for Ford. Within days, more than 4 million people visited Ford dealers across the country and purchased all 22,500 Mustangs. Within three months, Ford sold a record 100,000 Mustangs. Other automakers, hoping to capitalize on the fad, drew up plans for their own version of the Mustang. By 1967, the roadways of America were dominated by four-seat, large-engine "muscle cars" such as the Pontiac GTO, the Dodge Charger, and the Chevrolet Camaro.

Surfing became a fad during the 1960s thanks to the popularity of surf music and surfer movies, and to the fact that surfing symbolized freedom in the popular consciousness.

East Coast for fun in the sun in Southern California. And surfing was romanticized, even among the nonsurfing public, because it represented freedom. As Frederick Wardy wrote in *Surfer* magazine, "Surfing is a release from [the] exploding tensions of twentieth-century living. . . . [It is an] escape from the hustling, bustling city world of steel and concrete, a return to nature's reality." [89]

Although some people in California considered surfers to be bums who would rather wait for the perfect wave than get a good job, surfers were treated like big stars on the East Coast. When a surfing demonstration was given in New Jersey in 1965, more than seventy thousand people showed up to watch. This has been attributed to the idealized Hollywood image of the surfer, as Jane and Michael Stern explain:

The surfing craze that blossomed between 1961 and 1965 distilled California beach life to a sunshiny essence. It wasn't only about the sport of wave riding; it was a whole carefree cosmology of twanging guitars, hotrod cars, the smells of suntan lotion and sizzling cheeseburgers at an oceanside drive-in, and girls in bikinis and guys in tight white Levi's dancing the twist and the surfer stomp on Muscle Beach. The image of surfing swelled into a way of life, a point of view, a pose. The surfer transformed from a vaguely irresponsible beachcomber into a lifestyle pioneer who had discovered the holy grail of the decade: a fountain of eternal youth, represented by the ocean's waves and a sun that always shone.

The surfer who captured the imagination of the world in the early sixties was a physical ideal: lanky; sun-bleached . . . blond hair; skin that was tan . . . pale, dreamy eyes with sun-bleached brows . . . and an attitude. He was cool and he knew it. . . . Surfers were vitality personified, with their young muscles glistening in the salt spray and their round-the-clock search for pleasure. . . . They lived in a different universe than that of the brooding [beatniks] with their furrow-browed worries about the [atom] bomb and civil rights. They lived to party.[90]

Sidewalk Surfing

For those who could not make it out into the wild ocean waves, sidewalk surfing was the next best thing. And by 1965, people from San Diego to Bangor, Maine, were cruising their sidewalks with skateboards.

Kids had been making makeshift skateboards for decades by nailing roller skates onto chunks of wood. In the early sixties, a few imaginative skateboarders began making improvements to this crude toy. They used thin plastic instead of a board and mounted the wheels in such a way that a rider could change direction by shifting his weight from side to side, just like a wave surfer. Savvy toy makers recognized a fad in the making, and a new sport was born. In 1963, the first commercially produced skateboards, named Surf Skater, Makaha, and Bun Buster, appeared in Southern California stores. By 1965, skateboards were sold nationally, most for less than $3,

Many youngsters without access to the ocean took up sidewalk surfing, or skateboarding.

although a motorized version could cost $50. That year, manufacturers sold $30 million worth of skateboards.

As more young people picked up skateboards, a few talented riders began mastering jumps, obstacle courses, handstands, and other tricks. There was also controversy: After several children were injured in traffic, cities in Massachusetts, New York, California, and elsewhere banned skateboards from public thoroughfares. Although untold thousands of riders suffered bruises and broken bones, sidewalk surfing never went out of style.

The Hair Rebellion

The influence of the burgeoning youth culture did more than make toy makers rich. As the baby boomers entered their rebellious teen years, fashion statements such as long hair and love beads became a way of expressing personal identity—with a side benefit of upsetting parents and authorities.

The hair rebellion can be traced to the day in February 1964 when the Beatles performed on *The Ed Sullivan Show*. Band members wore their "mop-top" hair in long bangs down to their eyebrows. Their hair was shaggy on the sides, barely touching their ears, and long in back, grazing the collars of their shirts. At that time, this was considered outrageously long hair for men, and some adults were aghast. Young people, however, were entranced, and the appearance of the young American male changed practically overnight. As fashion historian Michael Sones writes on the Beauty Worlds website:

> I remember being in the schoolyard the day after the Beatles' appearance on Ed Sullivan and the talk was not of their music but how they shook their heads and how their hair flew in every direction. It was rebellious, it was wild, and it was free.[91]

Within days of the Beatles' appearance, countless young men began to let their hair grow over their ears and into long bangs. Those who were unable to grow long hair bought "Beatle wigs" which were selling by the thousands. Suddenly hair became a

During the 1960s, many young men grew their hair long as a symbol of youth and disobedience.

symbol of youth and rebellion, a form of disobedience that enraged people. Teenage boys with long hair were expelled from school or forced to cut their hair. In some areas long-haired boys were attacked and beaten.

Despite the risks and hassles, men grew their hair longer and longer as the decade progressed. Some had long hair flowing down past their shoulders, others wore untamed mops of curls sticking up atop their heads. All manner of beards, mustaches, and sideburns were also seen. Sones explains factors responsible for this trend:

[Wild], free long hair expressed the dissatisfaction of many with the materialism and consumerism of the culture and the Vietnam War, the Cold War, and the technology of what was called the military-industrial complex. Alienation became one of the buzzwords of the decade. Many people, especially the young, yearned for something else. It was time for a return to Nature. It was the dawning of hope and the Age of Aquarius. It would be a new beginning of community, love, and peace. The musical [play] *Hair* epitomized these values—wild, long, curly, flowing, free, blowin' in the wind, and hair down to our knees. The long hair . . . shocking for the time, symbolized an idealization of humans in the natural state. [92]

Even as many chose to get back to nature, the Beatles continued to set fashion trends. In 1967, the band released the album *Sgt. Pepper's Lonely Hearts Club Band*. The cover photo showed the Beatles as if they had been transformed into another group altogether—Sgt. Pepper's Lonely Hearts Club Band. The group wore brightly colored uniforms modeled on those worn by marching bands at the turn of the century. Their hair had also changed. The group wore thin mustaches and "shag" haircuts in which thin strands of hair were cut at various lengths. This look, much neater than wild hippie hair, was adopted by millions of men, from businessmen to rock musicians.

Of course there was a backlash to all this hairy rebellion. In some areas, billboards and bumper stickers proclaimed "Keep America Beautiful—Get a Haircut." [93] And in August 1969, when a group of Yippies! invaded Disneyland, rioted on Main Street, and occupied Tom Sawyer Island, the Disney company cracked down on long hair. The next day, Disneyland instituted strict grooming standards. Men with long hair were barred from the amusement park.

Shocking Fashion Statements

Just as hair continued to grow unchecked, fashion also got wilder as the decade progressed. In 1965, English designer Mary Quant began marketing the miniskirt with a hemline well above the knee. Until this time, women had rarely shown so much leg, and the skirt shocked authorities and religious leaders who associated the style with the sexual revolution. Quant, however, believed her skirt was about liberation, saying, "I wanted

Mary Quant (far right) began marketing the miniskirt in 1965. Many women of the 1960s wore the miniskirt and other racy fashions as a statement of their feminist ideology.

everyone to retain the grace of a child and not have to become stilted, confined, ugly beings. . . . So I created clothes that . . . allowed people to run, to jump, to leap, to retain their precious freedom."[94]

The miniskirt also freed women from garter belts. These elastic belts, long used to hold up stockings, could not be worn with miniskirts. Stocking manufacturers reacted by inventing panty hose, sheer tights that were worn like pants. Quant added patterns to panty hose that complemented the miniskirt. These too became an instant fad. By the early 1970s, 95 percent of all hosiery sold in the United States was of the panty-hose variety.

Women also began to wear shocking fashions to the beach. The bikini bathing suit, first seen on French fashion runways in the late 1940s, had become a standard outfit on American shores by the 1960s. Like so many other sixties fads, the bikini craze was triggered by rock music. In 1960, Brian Hyland had a hit with the novelty song "Itsy Bitsy Teenie Weenie Yellow Polka Dot Bikini," which set off a bikini-buying spree among American teens. By 1963, the bikini was the main form of female attire seen in surfer movies, further cementing the fad's place in American history. And in line with the 1960's audacity, the bikini was taken one step further in order to shock middle-class America.

In 1964, fashion designer Rudi Gernreich invented the one-piece topless bathing suit. While few women ever wore one in public—only three thousand were sold—the bathing suit did appear on the pages of *Life* magazine. This was free publicity that generated millions of dollars for Gernreich's other fashions.

Counterculture Fashions

By the late sixties, hippies did not need to bother wearing topless bathing suits, as they cavorted naked at Human Be-Ins and rock music festivals. Fashion had become what some were calling "anti-fashion,"[95] as members of the counterculture endeavored to retain a sense of childlike freedom.

Hippie fashions grew out of the acid tests that began in 1965. People attended those wild parties dressed as cowboys, Indians, pirates, Victorian housewives, English royalty, superheroes, 1920s flappers, and gypsies. They found these outfits at secondhand-clothing stores, costume rental shops, and in their grandparents' attics. And the dressing up was done more for fun than fashion, as designer Linda Gravenites states:

> People [at the acid tests] dressed no more bizarrely than they would to walk down Haight Street. . . . We were dressing up to go have a grand time and to be looked at, but mostly to please ourselves. That was what was so exciting. No purpose, no ulterior motive to getting dressed except fun. It's pleasurable to look strange or beautiful or medieval or American Indian.[96]

Like many other fashions of the sixties, hippie dress came to represent something more than just clothes. By then blue jeans were routine attire, no longer worn predominantly by farmers, coal miners, and other hardworking men. Members of the counterculture believed that when they wore jeans they were rejecting middle-class values by taking up the clothing of the working class (while avoiding the reality of backbreaking work). Dressing as Native Americans was seen as a way to show solidarity with a minority that had been horribly oppressed by white civilization for centuries, as the Sterns write:

> Although virtually all of them were Caucasian, hippies relished their romantic self-image as nouveau [Indians], living in harmony with the universe, fighting against the white man's perverted society of pollution, war, and greed. The hippie style . . . was like a version of Indian life from some old Hollywood movie, in which the long-haired tribesmen in buckskin fringe sit around their tepees smoking pipes, beating tom-toms, and speaking in [self-important] homilies, while the [women] . . . tend the babies and make dinner.[97]

Similarly, bells, love beads, headbands, and long robes were seen as emblems of outside cultures that were believed to be purer, and hence superior to modern America.

African American fashions also underwent major changes in the 1960s. The

Clothing with Psychedelic Color

The practice of dyeing cloth that had been tied in various patterns dates back thousands of years in India, Japan, and China. In the 1960s, however, tie-dye became a widespread fashionable phenomenon, as Richard A. Johnson writes in American Fads:

A simple home-stewing [tie-dye] procedure resulted in clothing and other fabric that fit the utilitarian, yet expressionist life style of sixties youth. The faintly geometric splotches of color and form were endlessly original and suggested the psychedelic experience derived from hallucinogenic drugs.

The hippie communities of San Francisco began do-it-yourself dyeing in 1966 and 1967 as the counterculture movement was taking shape. Rock musicians were soon wearing dye-patterned clothes onstage and by late 1969, tie-dye adorned young people throughout the country.

Tie-dyed goods could be purchased from artisans or cooked up at home. Using strands of tie string or elastic and boiling pots of dye, one could emblazon clothes, bedspreads, sheets, tablecloths, bath towels, curtains, and even create artwork suitable for framing. . . .

At the peak of the craze, some hippie households were awash in tie-dye. Everything from wall hangings and throw rugs to long johns and tennis shoes were being soaked in dye pots. Pop singer John Sebastian outfitted his entire house and body with wild flora from pots that steamed on his kitchen stove. . . . With popularity spreading to young people in every part of the country, major fabric producers . . . were mass-producing tie-dye designs for retail stores.

vividly colored African dashiki, made of loosely draped silk, was seen as a symbol of black pride. So too was the "afro" hairstyle, unprocessed or tightly curled hair in a round, full shape as high as it would grow. The Black Panthers' military-style clothing was also widely imitated by young men—and some women—in black neighborhoods. The Panther uniform consisted of black leather jackets, blue shirts, black trousers, and black berets.

Part of the Common Culture

Fashion statements of the sixties were popularized by individuals who had a strong desire, in the jargon of the times, to "do their own thing." By the late sixties, however, many hippie fashions had become part of the mainstream. And even as the baby boomers become senior citizens, their fashion statements, once considered shocking, have become as commonplace as blue jeans and tie-dyed T-shirts.

Notes

Chapter 1: A Revolution in Music

1. Quoted in Linda Martin and Kerry Segrave, *Anti-Rock*. Hamden, CT: Archon, 1988, p. 44.
2. Jane Stern and Michael Stern, *Sixties People*. New York: Knopf, 1990, p.103.
3. Quoted in David Hajdu, *Positively 4th Street*. New York: North Point 2001, pp. 116–17.
4. Quoted in Hajdu, *Positively 4th Street*, p. 118.
5. Quoted in David P. Szatmary, *Rockin' in Time: A Social History of Rock and Roll*. New York: Schirmer, 2000, p. 89.
6. Quoted in Hajdu, *Positively 4th Street*, p. 211.
7. Stern and Stern, *Sixties People*, pp. 114–15.
8. Quoted in Szatmary, *Rockin' in Time*, pp. 130–31.
9. Michael Gray, *Song & Dance Man III*. London: Cassell, 2000, p. 4.
10. Hajdu, *Positively 4th Street*, p. 234.
11. Quoted in Szatmary, *Rockin' in Time*, p 147.
12. Quoted in Szatmary, *Rockin' in Time*, p. 152.
13. Quoted in Szatmary, *Rockin' in Time*, p. 151.
14. Alice Echols, *Scars of Sweet Paradise*. New York: Metropolitan, 1999, p. 306.

Chapter 2: Art for the Commercial Age

15. Quoted in Time-Life Books, *Turbulent Years: The 60s*. Alexandria, VA: Time-Life, 1998, p. 42.
16. Quoted in Time-Life Books, *Turbulent Years*, p.42.
17. The Andy Warhol Homepage, "The Andy Warhol Biography" www.warhol.dk.
18. Quoted in Andrew J. Edelstein, *The Pop Sixties*. New York: World Almanac, 1985, p. 186.
19. Quoted in Gerald Howard, ed., *The Sixties: Art, Politics, and Media of Our Most Explosive Decade*. New York: Paragon House, 1991, p. 262.
20. Tom Wolfe, *Painted Word*. New York: Farrar, Straus and Giroux, 1975, p. 86.
21. Quoted inLinda Rosen Obst, ed., *The Sixties*. New York: Rolling Stone Press, 1977.
22. Paul Richard and Phil Ponce, "Remembering Roy Lichtenstein," PBS.org, 2003. www.pbs.org.
23. Quoted in Hugh Adams, *Art of the Sixties*. Oxford, England: Phaidon Press, Ltd. 1978, p. 54.
24. Quoted in Szatmary, *Rockin' in Time*, p. 153.

25. Szatmary, *Rockin' in Time,* pp. 153–54.
26. Sally Tomlinson and Walter Medeiros, *High Societies.* San Diego: San Diego Museum of Art, 2001, p. 21.
27. Quoted in Szatmary, *Rockin' in Time,* p. 154.
28. Tomlinson and Medeiros, *High Societies,* p. 21.
29. Tomlinson and Medeiros, *High Societies,* pp. 23–24.
30. Quoted in Reiko Tomii and Kathleen M. Friello, *Yes Yoko Ono.* New York: Harry N. Abrams, 2000, p. 28.
31. Quoted in Tomii and Friello, *Yes Yoko Ono,* p. 58.
32. Tomii and Friello, *Yes Yoko Ono,* p. 172.
33. Tomii and Friello, *Yes Yoko Ono,* p. 190.

Chapter 3: The Power of the Written Word

34. Philip D. Beidler, *Scriptures for a Generation: What We Were Reading in the 1960s.* Athens: University of Georgia Press, 1994, pp. 6–7.
35. Sudhi Rajiv, *Forms of Black Consciousness.* New York: Advent, 1992, p. 115.
36. Beidler, *Scriptures for a Generation,* p. 60.
37. Eldridge Cleaver, *Soul on Ice.* New York: Dell, 1968, p. 211.
38. Cleaver, *Soul on Ice,* p. xiii.
39. Cleaver, *Soul on Ice,* p. 134.
40. CNN.com, "He Was a Symbol: Eldridge Cleaver Dies at Age 62," May 1,1998. www.cnn.com.
41. Abbie Hoffman, *The Best of Abbie Hoffman.* New York: Four Walls Eight Windows, 1989, p. 30.
42. Hoffman, *The Best of Abbie Hoffman,* p. 77.
43. Hoffman, *The Best of Abbie Hoffman,* pp. 50–51.
44. Quoted in Beidler, *Scriptures for a Generation,* p. 109.
45. Joseph Heller, *Catch-22.* New York: Simon and Schuster, 1961, p. 45.
46. Quoted in Martin A. Lee and Bruce Shlain, *Acid Dreams.* New York: Grove Weidenfeld, 1992, p. 119.
47. Beidler, *Scriptures for a Generation,* p. 115.
48. Beidler, *Scriptures for a Generation,* p. 114.
49. Quoted in Barry G Cole, *Television.* New York: Free, 1970, p. 99.
50. Quoted in Cole, *Television,* p. 268.
51. Helen Gurley Brown, *Sex and the Single Girl.* New York: Bernard Geis, 1962, pp. 5–6.

Chapter 4: Stage and Screen

52. John Kenrick, "1960's Part III: The World Turned Upside Down," Musicals101.com, 2003. www.musicals101.com.
53. Theodore Shank, *American Alternative Theatre.* New York: Grove, 1982, p. 4.
54. Shank, *American Alternative Theatre,* p. 3.
55. Shank, *American Alternative Theatre,* p. 52.
56. Peter Biskind, *Easy Riders, Raging Bulls,* New York: Simon and Schuster, 1998, p. 20.

57. Edelstein, *The Pop Sixties*, p. 142.
58. Seth Cagin and Philip Dray, *Born to Be Wild*. Boca Raton, FL: Coyote, 1994, pp. 13–14.
59. Douglas Brode, *The Films of the Sixties*. Secaucus, NJ: Citadel, 1980, p. 279.
60. Quoted in Cagin and Dray, *Born to Be Wild*, p. 47.
61. Brode, *The Films of the Sixties*, pp. 287–88.
62. Quoted in Cagin and Dray, *Born to Be Wild*, p. 73.
63. Edelstein, *The Pop Sixties*, p. 152.
64. Biskind, *Easy Riders, Raging Bulls*, p. 14.

Chapter 5: Television Comes of Age

65. Quoted in Cole, *Television*, pp. 411–12.
66. Quoted in Lynn Spigel and Michael Curtin, eds., *The Revolution Wasn't Televised*. New York: Routledge, 1997, p. 3.
67. John Javna and Gordon Javna, *60s!* New York: St. Martin's, 1983, pp. 46–47.
68. David Farber, *The Great Age of Dreams: America in the 1960s*. New York: Hill and Wang, 1994, pp. 53–54.
69. Stern and Stern, *Sixties People*, pp. 219–20.
70. Stern and Stern, *Sixties People*, p. 220.
71. Adam Blair, "Your Thoughts on Bewitched," Harpies Bizare. www.harpiesbizarre.com.
72. Tom Hayden, *Reunion: A Memoir*. New York: Random House, 1988, p. 114.
73. Quoted in Javna and Javna, *60s!*, p. 82.
74. Quoted in Spigel and Curtin, *The Revolution Wasn't Televised*, p. 203.
75. Quoted in Spigel and Curtin, *The Revolution Wasn't Televised*, p. 205.
76. Quoted in Spigel and Curtin, *The Revolution Wasn't Televised*, p. 206.
77. Quoted in Javna and Javna, *60s!*, p. 58.
78. J. Fred MacDonald, *Blacks and White TV*. Chicago: Nelson-Hall, 1983, p. 108.
79. MacDonald, *Blacks and White TV*, p. 107.
80. Cole, *Television*, p. 252.
81. MacDonald, *Blacks and White TV*, p. 111.
82. Quoted in MacDonald, *Blacks and White TV*, p. 116.
83. MacDonald, *Blacks and White TV*, p. 115.
84. Quoted in Spigel and Curtin, *The Revolution Wasn't Televised*, p. 17.

Chapter 6: Toys, Fads, and Fashion

85. Quoted in Kristin Riddick, "Barbie: The Image of Us All." Inventing Barbie, www.people.virginia.edu.
86. Riddick, "Barbie: The Image of Us All."
87. Richard A. Johnson, *American Fads*. New York: Beech Tree, 1985, p. 82.
88. Johnson, *American Fads*, p. 83.

89. Quoted in Stern and Stern, *Sixties People,* pp. 79–80.
90. Stern and Stern, *Sixties People,* p. 80.
91. Michael Sones, "Hair in the 1960's," Beauty Worlds, May 2003. http://beauty.about.com.
92. Sones, "Hair in the 1960's."
93. Quoted in Sones, "Hair in the 1960's."
94. Quoted in Joel Lobenthal, *Radical Rags: Fashions of the Sixties.* New York: Abbeville, 1990, p. 11.
95. Time-Life Books, *Turbulent Years,* p. 172.
96. Quoted in Lobethal, *Radical Rags,* p. 114.
97. Stern and Stern, *Sixties People,* pp. 164, 166.

For Further Reading

Books

The Beatles, *The Beatles Anthology*. San Francisco: Chronicle, 2000. Four hundred large-format pages of rare photos and insightful text by the Beatles about the Beatles. As the book's dustcover says "The Beatles' story told for the first time in their own words and pictures."

Andrew J. Edelstein, *The Pop Sixties*. New York: World Almanac, 1985. A witty and irreverent look at the cultural icons of the sixties including fashion, music, television, film, and cars.

Stuart A. Kallen, *Life in America During the 1960s*. San Diego: Lucent, 2001. An examination of sixties American culture including suburbia, soldiers, Black Panthers, hippies, and liberated women.

Kitty Powe-Temperley, *The 60's: Mods & Hippies*. Milwaukee, WI: Gareth Stevens, 2000. Sixties fashion trends including miniskirts and Eastern and counterculture influences, with dozens of full-color photographs.

Michael A. Schuman, *Bob Dylan: The Life and Times of an American Icon*. Berkeley Heights, NJ: Enslow, 2003. A biography of one of the most innovative and creative songwriters of the twentieth century.

Sally Tomlinson and Walter Medeiros, *High Societies*. San Diego: San Diego Museum of Art, 2001. A book with striking reproductions of psychedelic posters from the 1960s-era Haight-Ashbury district.

Internet Sources

Tony Bove, Allen Cohen, and Raechel Donahue, "Rockument: Rock Music History," Rockument. www.rockument.com.

Mark Long, "Troll Dolls," Bad Fads, 2000. www.badfads.com.

Works Consulted

Books

Hugh Adams, *Art of the Sixties*. Oxford, England: Phaidon, 1978. A study of the explosion of artistic expression in New York and London and how the ideas were quickly spread around the world via the international media.

Philip D. Beidler, *Scriptures of Generation: What We Were Reading in the 1960s*. Athens: University of Georgia Press, 1994. A scholarly work that explores how best-selling books of the sixties examined war, racism, sexism, and other important issues.

Peter Biskind, *Easy Riders, Raging Bulls*. New York: Simon and Schuster, 1998. A book that explores how sex, drugs, and rock and roll swept through Hollywood in the late sixties and influenced the way producers, directors, and actors created films.

Douglas Brode, *The Films of the Sixties*. Secaucus, NJ: Citadel, 1980. A year-by-year study of sixties movies with stories, casts, and notes about the filming of the picture.

Helen Gurley Brown, *Sex and the Single Girl*. New York: Bernard Geis, 1962. The manifesto for the single sixties "perky" girl with tips on food, fashion, dating, romance, and catching a man.

Seth Cagin and Philip Dray, *Born to Be Wild*. Boca Raton, FL: Coyote, 1994. An exploration of sixties Hollywood films and how the movies depicted new attitudes toward racism, war, drugs, sex, and other social issues.

Eldridge Cleaver, *Soul on Ice*. New York: Dell, 1968. An influential dissection of black and white life in sixties America written in prison by a leading black revolutionary.

Barry G. Cole, *Television*. New York: Free, 1970. Reprints of articles that appeared in *TV Guide* magazine in the 1960s. Topics include the quality of the news, political coverage, programming, advertising, minorities on screen, censorship, and the effects of TV on society.

Anthony DeCurtis and James Henke with Holly George-Warren, eds., *The Rolling Stone Illustrated History of Rock*. New York: Random House, 1992. A definitive history of rock music with profiles by top rock critics of the most important artists and musical styles.

Alice Echols, *Scars of Sweet Paradise*. New York: Metropolitan, 1999. An exploration of how blues singer Janis Joplin re-created herself as a sixties rock and roll superstar after leaving her small Texas town as a beatnik folksinger.

David Farber, *The Great Age of Dreams: America in the 1960s.* New York: Hill and Wang, 1994. A history of the 1960s written from the perspective of the commonly held vision of the American dream and how the Vietnam War, rise of the counterculture, big-city riots, and other sixties conflicts disrupted that dream.

Gillian G. Gaar, *She's a Rebel.* Seattle: Seal, 1992. The history of women in rock and roll from the 1950s to the 1990s.

Martin Gottfried, *Opening Nights: Theater Criticism of the Sixties.* New York: G.P. Putnam's Sons, 1969. A collection of New York City theater criticism by the senior critic who worked for *Women's Wear Daily* from 1963 to mid-1969.

Michael Gray, *Song & Dance Man III.* London: Cassell, 2000. A weighty and intellectual assessment of Bob Dylan songs with analysis of his lyrics and much speculation about the singer's various motives and inspirations.

David Hajdu, *Positively 4th Street.* New York: North Point, 2001. A book that traces the influences of folksingers Joan Baez, her sister Mimi Farina, Bob Dylan, and songwriter Richard Farina, on popular music and literature in the first half of the 1960s.

Tom Hayden, *Reunion: A Memoir.* New York: Random House, 1988. An autobiography by a man who was one of the founding members of the Students for a Democratic Society, led dozens of protests in the sixties, and was put on trial for conspiracy after the Chicago Democratic Convention. Hayden later went on to marry actress Jane Fonda and served many years as a state assemblyman in California.

Joseph Heller, *Catch-22.* New York: Simon and Schuster, 1961. The leading antiwar novel of the 1960s uses dark humor to expose horrors of war and the absurdity of military bureaucracy.

Abbie Hoffman, *The Best of Abbie Hoffman.* New York: Four Walls Eight Windows, 1989. A compilation of Yippie! founder Abbie Hoffman's best writing over the years including excerpts from his groundbreaking books *Revolution for the Hell of It, Woodstock Nation,* and *Steal This Book.* Also included are newer articles written in the 1980s.

———, *Revolution for the Hell of It.* New York: Dial, 1968. Published under the pseudonym "Free," this book describes Hoffman's antiwar and anticapitalism antics as leader of the Yippie! party.

Barney Hoskyns, *Beneath the Diamond Sky: Haight-Ashbury 1965–1970.* New York: Simon and Schuster, 1997. A book with dozens of photographs and rainbow-colored pages that describe the social, cultural, political, and musical scene in America's premier hippie neighborhood during the late sixties.

Gerald Howard, ed., *The Sixties: Art, Politics, and Media of Our Most Explosive Decade.* New York: Paragon

House, 1991. A collection of essays by well-known writers such as Norman Mailer, Susan Sontag, and Tom Wolfe that explore the art, politics, and media of the turbulent sixties.

John Javna and Gordon Javna, *60s!* New York: St. Martin's, 1983. A book about the popular culture of the sixties illustrated with hundreds of photos of cars, fashions, comics, toys, movie posters, album covers, baseball cards, television stills, and more.

Richard A. Johnson, *American Fads*. New York: Beech Tree, 1985. A study of fads embraced by Americans between the 1950s and the 1980s, including goldfish swallowing, hula hoops, troll dolls, mood rings, and pet rocks.

Martin A. Lee and Bruce Shlain, *Acid Dreams*. New York: Grove Weidenfeld, 1992. A book that explores the social history of LSD from the CIA's 1950s attempt to use it as a secret weapon to the widespread use of the drug during the hippie era of the 1960s. The authors unearthed twenty thousand documents from secret government files in order to paint a startling picture of the CIA's involvement in one of the largest public drug experiments in history.

Joel Lobenthal, *Radical Rags: Fashions of the Sixties*. New York: Abbeville, 1990. An illustrated exploration of fashions as they were influenced by social trends from London and New York to Haight-Ashbury.

J. Fred MacDonald, *Blacks and White TV*. Chicago: Nelson-Hall, 1983. A study of the roles African Americans played on television from the medium's earliest days.

Malcolm X with Alex Haley, *The Autobiography of Malcolm X*. New York: Ballantine, 1990. The life story of one of the most famous and charismatic leaders of the black power revolution.

George Martin, *With a Little Help from My Friends: The Making of Sgt. Pepper*. New York: Little, Brown, 1994. Details the technical and creative processes behind the Beatles' most highly acclaimed masterpiece written by the producer who was instrumental in shaping those sounds.

Linda Martin and Kerry Segrave, *Anti-Rock*. Hamden, CT: Archon, 1988. A history of the resistance to, and censorship of, rock music by politicians, clergy, parents, and law-enforcement authorities.

Lynda Rosen Obst, ed., *The Sixties*. New York: Rolling Stone Press, 1977. A year-by-year summary of the 1960s in the words of well-known writers, musicians, actors, and activists of the decade.

Sudhi Rajiv, *Forms of Black Consciousness*. New York: Advent, 1992. An analysis of the political, religious, and intellectual thought expressed in books by Malcolm X, Eldridge Cleaver, and others.

Jerry Rubin, *Do It!* New York: Ballantine, 1970. One of the most radical books of the sixties, written by the founder of the Yippies! He tells students to drop out, resist authority, and foment revolution against schools, government, corporations, and society. *Do It!* traces Rubin's life from a straight-laced sports reporter to a revolutionary agitator against the Vietnam War in the late sixties.

Arthur Sainer, *The Radical Theatre Notebook*. New York: Discus, 1975. An overview of politically and socially motivated theater companies that performed from the 1950s to the mid-1970s.

Theodore Shank, *American Alternative Theater*. New York: Grove, 1982. The history of nontraditional theater between the 1950s and the 1980s by a professor of dramatic art at the University of California.

June Sochen, *Herstory*. New York: Knopf, 1974. The author, a professor of history at Northwestern University, presents the women's side of American history and details the life stories and experiences of women who helped make the United States the successful country it is today.

Lynn Spigel and Michael Curtin, eds., *The Revolution Wasn't Televised*. New York: Routledge, 1997. Essays by various authors, experts, and critics about the influence of sixties television on social movements and cultural conflict.

Jane Stern and Michael Stern, *Sixties People*. New York: Knopf, 1990. An entertaining book that covers the unique cultural trappings of surfers, folk singers, hippies, rebels, "Mr. and Mrs. Average," and other character types of the 1960s.

David P. Szatmary, *Rockin' in Time: A Social History of Rock and Roll*. New York: Schirmer, 2000. A social history of rock and roll that focuses on the African American contributions to the style, from its ancient tribal roots to hip-hop.

Time-Life Books, *Turbulent Years: The 60s*. Alexandria, VA: Time-Life, 1998. A big, colorful volume that covers all aspects of 1960s culture including the war in Vietnam, assassinations, hippies, communes, rock and roll, and the antiwar movement.

Reiko Tomii and Kathleen M. Friello, *Yes Yoko Ono*. New York: Harry N. Abrams, 2000. A richly illustrated book that spans the innovative artist's entire career and explores her contributions to art, film, and music.

Tom Wolfe, *Painted Word*. New York: Farrar, Straus and Giroux, 1975. An amusing critique of twentieth-century artists, galleries, and the art-buying public.

Periodical

Anthony DeCurtis, "Sam Phillips," *Rolling Stone*, September 4, 2003. A tribute to Sam Phillips, the founder of Sun Records, who started the rock and roll revolution by producing the records of B.B. King, Elvis Presley, Johnny Cash, Ike Turner, and others.

Internet Sources

The Andy Warhol Homepage, "The Andy Warhol Biography." www.warhold.dk.

Adam Blair, "Your Thoughts on Bewitched," Harpies Bizarre. www.harpiesbizarre.com.

CNN.com, "He Was a Symbol: Eldridge Cleaver Dies at Age 62," May 1, 1998. www.cnn.com.

Sara Ironman, "Diane Arbus," The Photography of Diane Arbus. www.temple.edu.

John Kenrick, "1960's Part II: A Golden Era Ends," Musicals101.com, 2003. www.musicals101.com.

———, "1960's Part III: The World Turned Upside Down," Musicals 101.com, 2003. www.musicals101.com.

Jean H. Lee, "Counterculture 'Comix' Reach Ripe Old Age," Southcoast Today.com, 1999. www.s-t.com.

Paul Richard and Phil Ponce, "Remembering Roy Lichtenstein," PBS.org, 2003. www.pbs.org

Kristin Riddick, "Barbie: The Image of Us All." Inventing Barbie, www.people.virginia.edu.

Michael Sones, "Hair in the 1960's," Beauty Worlds, May 2003. http://beauty.about.com.

Jack Valenti, "How It All Began," MPA, Movie Ratings, History, December 2000. www.mpaa.org.

Index

Picture Credits

Cover: © Hulton Archive by Getty Images
© Bettmann/CORBIS, 15, 31, 37, 43, 45, 52, 55, 57. 62, 72, 74, 81, 85, 91
© Jonathan Blair/CORBIS, 60
© Henry Diltz/CORBIS, 93
© Malcolm Lubliner/CORBIS, 7
© Wally McNamee/CORBIS, 75

© Ted Streshinsky/CORBIS, 34, 89
Hulton Archive/Getty Images, 10, 11, 12, 13, 16, 20, 21, 23, 24(both), 27, 28, 32, 40, 47, 49, 51, 67, 70, 71, 77, 92, 95
The Kobal Collection, 63, 66
Library of Congress, 41

About the Author

Stuart A. Kallen is the author of more than 170 nonfiction books for children and young adults. He has written on topics ranging from the theory of relativity to the history of rock and roll. In addition, Mr. Kallen has written award-winning children's videos and television scripts. In his spare time, Stuart A. Kallen is a singer/songwriter/guitarist in San Diego, California.